LITTLE PAT

THE RIDDLESWORTH EVACUEE MURDER

DARREN NORTON

Trigger Warning: Contains description of a murder of a young child.

Produced by Softwood Books, Suffolk, UK

Text © Darren Norton, 2024

First Edition

ISBN: 978-1-7385709-0-4

www.softwoodbooks.com

Dedicated to Patricia Ann Cupit
19th October 1935 – 6th May 1942
Buried in Streatham Park Cemetery, London

CONTENTS

PREFACE

Riddlesworth Park, on the Norfolk/Suffolk border presents a typical East Anglian landscape, offering wide open horizons across a flat grassland. Sporadic trees and shrubs form small wooded areas, from where roosting rooks squawk. Crossing the grassland, a dirt track, at least part way lined by reeds towering up from drainage ditches, is used by walkers and occasionally farming vehicles. Essentially, anyone walking along the track today will enjoy a landscape almost unchanged for over a century.

In the 1940s, compared to many places in Britain, it was a very serene and safe environment. The park was somewhere you might seek out for a quiet picnic. Occasionally, the sound of a vehicle driving along a distant country lane might be heard, its sound carried by a light breeze. The park was so safe that young children would walk across it, unaccompanied, to reach their school. Local residents lived in small hamlets of two or three cottages scattered around the park. If you know the story of the *Little House on the Prairie*, then it will give you an idea of the pace of life in Riddlesworth.

When war came to the area, it brought soldiers, their billets and their trucks. While other towns saw hundreds of evacuees require housing, Riddlesworth saw only seven, one of them being a 6-years-old girl from London. Patricia Ann Cupit stayed with a farmer and his wife, and by all accounts, 'Little Pat' as she was known, enjoyed her time with Albert and Flo Pask. Sometimes Flo would take Pat to school on her cycle, sometimes Pat would walk the journey on her own.

Then, one day, Pat failed to return home from school. It transpired she had never even arrived there. That evening her lifeless body was found under a tree, not too far from Riddlesworth Hall. Pat had been brutally stabbed with a knife and partially strangled. Although she was taken to hospital, she died in the early hours of the next day. The Norfolk Constabulary immediately investigated, but with the vast number of soldiers and residents scattered around the area, the task to interview them all was so immense that they contacted London's New Scotland Yard for assistance. Two detectives arrived the next day.

Hundreds were interviewed and, within a couple of weeks, someone confessed to the attack. In his subsequent trial at the Old Bailey, it was claimed he could not remember carrying it out, yet, also at the trial, his long history of offending against little girls was highlighted by the prosecution. The defence stated his previous actions showed a propensity toward being "not normal". Both sides brought medical experts to give evidence, in what was widely reported in the nation's newspapers. No one denied the accused had attacked the girl, the question was – was he insane when he did so? Herbert Morrison, Winston Churchill's Home Secretary, ordered the accused to be taken for a scan of his brainwaves, using new technology not widely available. The accused, upon being found guilty of murder, was sentenced to hang at the hands of Britain's most prolific executioner. However, this was still not the end of his story. There was an appeal. Ex-servicemen and mental health groups wanted their say. The Secretary of State ordered a statutory inquiry, backed by the weight of the law. Would the accused eventually hang?

The tree that Pat was found under still stands today. A public footpath, the 'Angles Way', passes within metres of where the attack took place. Yet it is doubtful any walkers are aware of the violence that was once metered out there, such is the idyllic setting. In contrast, Pat lay buried in an unmarked grave for 40 years, with her story all but forgotten. This book aims to honour the memory of Pat, and highlight the story that unfolded after she was attacked.

MAP OF RIDDLESWORTH PARK – May 1942

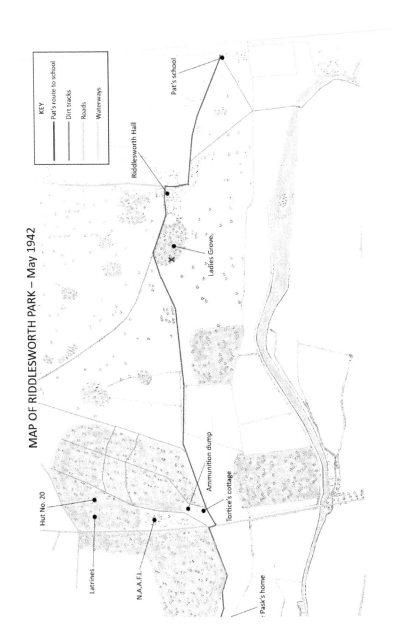

KEY
- Pat's route to school
- Dirt tracks
- Roads
- Waterways

Pat's school

Riddlesworth Hall

Ladies Grove

Ammunition dump

Tortice's cottage

Hut No. 20

Latrines

N.A.A.F.I.

Pask's home

Patricia Ann Cupit. Image courtesy of Anna Allan.

Leonard Cupit (left); Anne Cupit (right). Images courtesy of Anna Allan.

James Wyeth, 1940, image taken upon his entry into borstal.
Image reproduced under licence -TNA, PCOM9705.

PART ONE – THE INVESTIGATION

WEDNESDAY, 6TH MAY, 1942

Manchester Evening News – *Girl dies of wounds in throat. Aged 6½ years, a girl whose parents live at Riddlesworth, a village on the Norfolk and Suffolk border.*

Nottingham Evening Post – *Found dying of wounds … died in hospital from throat and other wounds inflicted by an unknown assailant.*

Belfast Telegraph – *Murdered little girl. Grim English crime … The child was found last night lying in a critical condition under bushes in a park at the village.*

Aberdeen Evening Express – *Child found dying. The police are making investigations.*

In May, 1942, few of the nation's newspaper readers have the least bit knowledge of where Riddlesworth is in the world, but that is all about to change. Today sees the first reports of a 6-years-old girl attacked there and left to die. Those initial reports are sketchy. The newspapers do not know the child's name, nor the exact location of the attack, although Riddlesworth is confirmed as being where it happened, and apparently the child's parents live in the village. What is certain is a young girl was stabbed in the throat and later died in hospital.

Norfolk County Constabulary were among the first on the scene and their investigation began immediately. However, they know their police force will be stretched, so at 5.45pm, their chief constable sends an urgent telegram to the Metropolitan Police, based in London. It reads:

"I would like the assistance of a Chief Inspector to investigate a case of murder which occurred yesterday near Thetford. Patricia Cupit, aged 6½ years, left home at 8.20am, 5th May, to go to school and about 5.50pm, the same day, she was found in a ditch near Thetford. The girl died in Bury St. Edmunds Hospital..."

THURSDAY, 7TH MAY, 1942

Western Daily Press – *Stabbed child dies. There were no signs of a struggle.*

Leicester Evening Mail – *Stabbed Girl. Hunt* **for the assailant** … *the child was found with a piece of old coconut matting partly thrown over her.*

Birmingham Mail – *Murdered little girl. The inquest will be opened today.*

Daily Mirror – Village darling evacuee murdered … *Detective Inspector Garner, of the Norfolk C.I.D., with a squad of men combed the district yesterday. Two officers from Scotland Yard will arrive today.*

It is 11.25am. A steam train from Cambridge pulls up alongside the eastbound platform at Thetford railway station, just inside the Norfolk county border with Suffolk. The train comes to a halt and passengers disembark, among them two dark-suited men step onto the platform. They are detectives, sent to the town to assist the police investigation into an horrific murder of a child. One of the men, Chief Inspector Thomas Barratt, is here to lead that investigation. Local police have little experience of dealing with an attack of such barbarity as this, nor have they had a case that has caught the imagination of the national press to such an extent. Newspapers across the UK are giving it column inches, where the story vies with updates of the war. Barratt knows he will be judged by how he handles such a high-profile case, so he is comforted by the confidence he has in his companion, Detective Sergeant Albert Webb, and the fact they have years of experience working within the Criminal Investigation Department of New Scotland Yard. Yet, this will be Barratt's first time leading an investigation. It will also be the first time the two detectives have been assigned to a case outside of London.

Barratt finds himself in unfamiliar surroundings. Thetford railway station, with its buildings of flint and red brick, serves the rural town of about 4,000 inhabitants and sits on the Cambridge to Norwich railway line. Three hours ago, Barratt departed from Liverpool Street station, leaving behind London's densely built streets, and he now stands on a station platform surrounded by allotments and a wide-open horizon. He spots three similarly well-dressed, official looking men, so presumes they are here to meet him. The most striking of the three is Stephen Van Neck, a moustached man with a distinguished military career in the Great War, and who, six years ago, led King George V's funeral procession from Sandringham. Van Neck knows about police protocol and yesterday, acting as Chief Constable of Norfolk County Constabulary, he sent a request to the chief of London's police force, asking for assistance. Just over a week ago, Van Neck's men had been dealing with the aftermath of a German aerial bombing raid on Norwich, a raid that would later be known as being part of the Baedeker Raids, so he knows this complex murder investigation will overstretch his county force should the enemy return and wreak more havoc. If possible, he needs a speedy resolution, therefore he can have no complaints about how quickly London responded. Van Neck is accompanied on the platform by two Norfolk colleagues, Detective Inspector William Garner and Superintendent Sidney Bushell. Barratt has seen Garner's name mentioned in the press, and he knows he will need to work closely with him if he is to pick up the case details quickly. The two groups converge and shake hands. There are introductions and, to anyone witnessing this, it does seem a very business-like and formal greeting. But then, of course, it is. With the greetings concluded, the men are conveyed from Thetford railway station to the town's police station, a distance of about half a mile. Within 20 minutes of stepping off the train, the two detectives are being briefed about their new investigation.

Just a few miles away, in a sparsely populated area known as Riddlesworth Park, there has been a most horrific murder. On Tuesday, 5th May, a 6½-years-old evacuee girl was brutally stabbed and strangled while on her way to school. The poor child did not die instantly, but instead managed to hang on to the slightest chance of life for a few hours until she passed away in hospital yesterday morning, her wounds too great to offer any real chance of recovery. Fewer than a hundred people normally live in the area of Riddlesworth Park, but this is wartime Norfolk, so there is a large transient population of troops and school staff, who live nearby. These people may be here today, but tomorrow they could be somewhere else. The Norfolk Constabulary know time is of the essence if they are to catch the person responsible. The detectives also consider another problem: there are no witnesses to the attack. Barratt is told nothing has been ruled in and nothing ruled out. However, he has learned from past experience that murders often occur between people known to each other. Barratt is briefed on what the local police have been up to in the hours following the attack. Statements have already been taken from those close to the child, from those who found the body and also from people who came forward to say they saw something suspicious, enabling the police to build up a background of the girl and her typical movements. They have also managed to take a handful of statements from soldiers billeted and working near the park that day.

THE EVACUEE GIRL, PATRICIA CUPIT

Leonard, a sergeant in the Royal Air Force, and Anne Cupit had been married for two years when their first born, a girl, was born on 19th October, 1935. They named her Patricia Anne Cupit, although she was often referred to as 'Pat', or 'Little Pat'. Together, the three of them lived at 1543a London Road, Norbury, London, S.W.16, until war was declared in September 1939.

The British Government, concerned that London was going to be a target for German bombers, not knowing if the enemy might even drop gas onto the capital's civilian population, sent children away from the city to areas considered relatively safe. The first day of evacuation was Friday 1st September, 1939, two days before Britain declared on Germany, with more evacuees sent away on the 2nd and 3rd. Against this backdrop, and with Pat considered by the authorities as being too young to travel unaccompanied on the Government scheme, her parents sought their own arrangements to send her to stay in a 'safe' area. Leonard, through family friends, found Pat such a place with someone who had connections to their home district of Norbury. William Hillier had moved from nearby Norwood after the Great War and, in 1939, was living with his wife at 15 Vale Road, Portslade, on the Sussex coast near Brighton. Mr Hillier, a police sergeant on the Southern Railway at Brighton, was someone the Cupits trusted. They therefore decided to send their daughter, who at that time had not reached the age of four, to stay with the couple.

Nonetheless, from September 1939 through April 1940, London was not attacked. Indeed, some of the children evacuated out of the city then returned home, although Pat stayed with the Hilliers, seemingly happy to do so. It was the fall of France, to the German army in June 1940, that made the Cupits re-consider the safety of their daughter. The enemy had just swept through Holland, Belgium and France at breathtaking speed, forcing those countries' collapse within weeks. Therefore, the threat of invasion along the south coast of Britain was a real one, especially where Pat was staying, near Brighton, which is nearer to the French coast than Paris is. Considering London had not been bombed by that time in the war, in August 1940, Pat's parents felt it safer to bring their daughter back into the city and away from the south coast. However, their daughter did not stay with them long, but instead lived three miles away with Leonard's mother, at 61 Tremain Road, Anerley, in south east London. There, Pat stayed in relative safety for a little over two months, but in September 1940, a year after war was declared, the German Luftwaffe systematically began bombing London. Pat's parents sought another place of sanctuary for their daughter, a process which took almost a year to conclude. Once again, the destination for their daughter was found through a friendship with a policeman, Detective Charles Baker, of the Criminal Investigation Department, at Norbury Police Station. Detective Baker's sister, Florence Pask, known as Flo, lived in a tiny village called Riddlesworth, just inside the Norfolk border with Suffolk, and about 100 miles north-east of Norbury. Although it was a place Leonard had never heard of, it was nonetheless probably a place the German bombers were unlikely to visit either. In August 1941, Pat was sent to stay with Flo and her husband, Albert. A couple of months later, Pat celebrated her sixth birthday with them.

By all accounts, Pat was very happy staying with the Pasks. Her parents regarded them as being Pat's 'foster parents', and Pat's mother would often pop up to Norfolk to visit her 'little Pat'. Following her visit, when Mrs Cupit returned to her husband in London, she talked of how cheerful her daughter had been. Pat would often write letters to her parents, sent by Mrs Pask, enabling them all to keep in touch regularly. At no time did Pat give a hint she was troubled. She was never sick and seemed to be developing as well as any other 6-years-old, in fact she was considered quite tall for her age. The last visit from Pat's parents was just four weeks before the attack, when her father called in. Again, he came away with the opinion she was very much loved by the Pasks. Just days before the murder, Pat wrote to her father,

Dear Daddy.

I shall be pleased to see you. I am a big girl now, I can read, skip, knit and tell the time. Do you like my real handwriting?

I shall be pleased with the chocolate. I haven't had any for a long time.

I am now going to bed so goodnight Daddy, with love from Pat. XXXXXXXXXXXXX

On the fateful day of 5th May, 1942, Pat woke up and had a breakfast of bread and milk, prepared for her by Mrs Pask, who also packed her a lunch of four sandwiches and a cake to take to school, placing it inside Pat's silver coloured handbag. At about 8.20am, Pat left the Pasks' home and set off for school. It was the last time they saw her alive.

That morning, it was a bright sunny day and Pat left the house wearing a green jumper under her pink coat, and on her head was a matching pink hat. A blue gymslip covered her to above her knees, and she wore brown socks in her brown shoes. From the Pasks' home, Pat would have walked about 300 yards to a narrow tarmac lane, with forest on her left and a field on her right, the field bordered by a low wooden fence. The road was hardly ever used, only by occasional local traffic, sometimes military trucks, so there was little danger to her when crossing this to resume her journey on the dirt track opposite. After crossing the road, the dirt track would have taken her all the way to school without seeing another road. She would pass only one house, just 50 metres away, on the left side of the dirt track. It was a brick and flint-built cottage, lived in by Mr Tortice, the caretaker of Riddlesworth Hall. His cottage, like that of the Pasks', looks out onto the open grassland of Riddlesworth Park. Behind Tortice's cottage are outbuildings sitting on the very edge of a forest that contains an Army camp housing over 300 soldiers who had been recently brought into the area. In fact, some had arrived just days earlier. A wooden fence marks the boundary of Tortice's cottage from the dirt track, and from another track that veers off into the forest, toward the Army camp.

Beyond Tortice's cottage, Pat's journey would have continued through the park, and after about 200 yards along the track, the woods on her left side gave way to open countryside. The only landmarks were the occasional small grouping of trees, shallow ditches and a few telegraph poles. From here, Pat would have got her first glimpse of Riddlesworth Hall, a landmark dominating the park. The huge house is three storeys tall, with stone steps leading up to an entrance flanked with pillars, a balustraded parapet decorates the roof and the rooms have high ceilings, as implied by the very tall windows throughout. Pat's walk then took her onto the grounds of the Hall, across the front driveway, passing the imposing front entrance of the Hall, round a corner past a church, and then onto another dirt track toward the hamlet of Gasthorpe. About half a mile down this track was her school. It is here, on the track from the Hall to the school, that the local postman, Charles Foreman, frequently passed Pat as he cycled along doing his delivery round. In a statement given to the police, he said he would often see her walking alone, but sometimes with an older lady, Mrs Pask. Although he never stopped or walked with them, he did nonetheless always acknowledge them, sometimes even engaging in conversation with young Pat as he passed by. Yet, on 5th May 1942, Pat did not walk that part of the track to school. She did not even pass Riddlesworth Hall. That day, her journey ended just before the Hall, at a place known locally as Ladies Grove. It was here she was attacked and her body dumped among a small group of trees and bushes. So far, the police had drawn a blank as to a motive or suspect.

On the fateful day of 5th May, 1942, Pat woke up and had a breakfast of bread and milk, prepared for her by Mrs Pask, who also packed her a lunch of four sandwiches and a cake to take to school, placing it inside Pat's silver coloured handbag. At about 8.20am, Pat left the Pasks' home and set off for school. It was the last time they saw her alive.

STATEMENTS
ALBERT PASK'S STATEMENT

Mr and Mrs Pask, of Stud Cottages, on the edge of Riddlesworth Park, have no children of their own and they are not wealthy by any stretch of the imagination. They lead a simple life in the Norfolk countryside, yet it is in a setting some may yearn for. The Pasks' home is about 300 yards down a dirt track, the track itself comes off a narrow country lane, so not much in the way of motorised traffic comes their way. Their modest cottage is set against a backdrop of the forest trees while overlooking Riddlesworth Park, and, with only a handful of other houses nearby, it is so isolated that surely anyone wanting to get away from the hustle and bustle of a busy town would seek this idyllic setting. However, this is a community of farm workers, not holiday retreats. Amenities are basic, mains electricity and water are yet to reach here and no one has a telephone installed. The setting also projects a place that is a million miles away from the war, one the enemy would have no benefit in attacking. In terms of location, on the surface of it, Pat's parents had chosen well.

Chief Inspector Barratt is told that the husband, Albert Pask, was also the one who discovered the child's body, which makes the man a key witness. Yesterday, not long after Pat had died in hospital, Detective Inspector William Garner, of Norfolk County Constabulary, visited Albert at his home to find out a bit more about the man, his relationship with Pat and his actions leading up to the discovery of the victim's body.

30-years-old Albert is married to Flo, with their home tied to his job as a labourer on a nearby farm. Detective Inspector Garner informs Barratt that during his visit to the Pasks, Albert came across as a fairly simple man, perhaps even below average intelligence. Garner also noted Albert was very nervous. Were these nerves because he had just experienced a very traumatic event? Discovering Pat lying close to death would challenge the strongest constitution of anyone, but she had been staying under his roof, so the stress on him must have been immense. Or was it the presence of the detective in his home? Even if it was the latter, again, a stranger in your home asking formal questions and writing down your answers, could challenge the best of us. Perhaps it was a combination of both scenarios? Barratt is handed Albert's version of events surrounding the day the child was attacked.

It seems Albert left home for work, at around 7.20am that morning. He noted Pat was still asleep in her bed, which was not unusual, so continued on to his place of work. At that point, it was just like any other ordinary day. It was only upon almost arriving home from work, late that afternoon, that he discovered Pat had not returned from school. It was at about 5.10pm, at the crossroads of the lane and dirt track near his home, when Albert met his wife. She looked anxious. She told him Pat had not yet returned from school, so they both hurried back home, where she grabbed her identity card and went cycling off to look for the child. Albert stayed behind, just in case Pat returned while his wife was out. When a young lad came by the house, Albert asked him if he had seen Pat, but the boy claimed he had not seen the girl whatsoever that day, not even at school. It was then Albert became most concerned, especially as Pat was always home before he was. She was known for getting distracted along her journey, sometimes making her late for school, but with confirmation she had not made it to school that day, Pat's disappearance had taken a more serious turn. So, Albert jumped on his cycle and also went looking, the young boy did likewise, following closely behind.

Albert cycled the route Pat would have taken that morning. From his home to the school, it was a distance of just over a mile of dirt tracks through Riddlesworth Park, while skirting around the grounds of Riddlesworth Hall. Pat's school was not much bigger than his own cottage, and was very modest in comparison to the grandeur of Riddlesworth Hall. In fact, it may have once belonged to the Riddlesworth Hall estate, and housed staff from the Hall. Upon arriving at the school, Albert was told by the governess that Pat had not attended that day. With no sighting of Pat since she left home, he decided this matter was now beyond him, so he sought to inform the police. He and the young lad left the governess and made their way back home. In hindsight, their journey to the school had been done in haste, meaning they had not taken much notice of their surroundings as they went, but on their way back their eyes scanned the park for any sign of the girl. Having left the school, they cycled back up the dirt track towards the Hall, flanked either side by hedgerows and farm land. They passed the church on their right, with its low wall and cemetery, then a tight right bend took them in front of the impressive Hall. Moments later, with the Hall behind them, they emerged onto the dirt track which would take them across the park and back home. At this point, on their left, was a small collection of trees, known locally as 'Ladies Grove'.

It was the young lad who made the discovery - a pink woollen hat lying in the grass, just to the left of the footpath, near to Ladies Grove. He alerted Albert, who got off his cycle to check it out. It was Pat's hat. Albert then ventured further under the low-lying branches and into the bushes, where he then saw the child's school bag. He could see it still had her lunch in it, not yet eaten. He carefully stepped further into the undergrowth, not sure of what he was going to find. Then, he caught a sight, one that filled his heart with dread. A child's leg protruded from under some dirty old coconut matting. Albert's eyes looked beyond the matting and instantly he recognised the child's face. It was covered with blood. His next reaction was probably down to shock, his brain unable to process what he may find if he moved the matting. Albert left the child's body - and ran. He ran across Riddlesworth Park, and towards the nearest place he thought he could get help, Riddlesworth Hall, where he had earlier heard girls playing on the sports field. Albert, in his confused state, undoubtedly trying to process what he had just seen, ran at the girls in their sports uniform, shouting and demanding to see their school governess. When she came to see him, he took her to where he had seen the child's body, perhaps to prove this was no hoax. He then asked her to go back to the Hall and use her telephone to alert the police and a doctor.

It was at this point Flo arrived and caught up with her husband. He was about to return into the bushes, so he explained to his wife what he had seen. Only then did they discover the child was still alive and breathing, although each breath seemed to involve a momentous effort. The child appeared to be in much pain and her body was still covered by the dirty matting, having laid undisturbed since being discovered. Albert, in his statement to Detective Inspector Garner said:

"*We did not touch Patricia and heard her breathing heavy. Her legs were apart, the matting came down to her knees. Her face was covered with the matting, her head was back and face pointing to the sky. When the doctor arrived and uncovered her, I saw her knickers were down to her knees.*"

Albert stayed at the scene until 7pm, when an ambulance arrived to take Pat to hospital. He told Garner the girl had been more than happy to stay with him and his wife. The feeling was mutual, they had no children of their own, so they treated her like their own daughter. Pat's mother had visited during the previous Christmas and the father had also come down since then, so it seemed the child's parents were more than happy with the arrangement too. Albert also claimed he had warned Pat not to talk to strangers, or get into any trucks with soldiers, while she was walking over the park. He felt she was unlikely to have gone against his advice, what with her being mature for her age. Although to some, allowing a 6-years-old to walk unsupervised the mile or so to school each day may on the surface appear to be inviting trouble, it was, in the countryside, nothing out of the ordinary. In fact, the child had never reported anything untoward up to that day.

Flo Pask was also visited by Garner after Pat was attacked. She confirmed the child had bread and milk for breakfast, a meal that took her 40 minutes to eat. It seems Pat was known to be a very slow eater. On the fateful day, Flo packed Pat a lunch of four sandwiches and a cake. Flo, as she always did, then kissed Pat goodbye and saw the girl walk down the track towards school. Flo said Pat would sometimes be taken to school on the back of her cycle, but often the child walked there alone. As far as Flo was aware, Pat had never mentioned anything about being harassed or frightened while she walked the route. In fact, she had said she was more than happy to walk to and from school unaccompanied. Flo said in her statement:

"She goes alone and there are no other children [who] go that way. The path is used by the general public. There are three cottages near ours and all the occupants use that path. The soldiers also used to use it. When I have taken her across that way walking, I have never met anybody. Patricia has never made any complaint to me about anyone stopping her or frightening her. She was not at all nervous."

Flo confirmed that when Pat had not returned home from school, she jumped on her cycle and went looking for her. She also confirmed when she returned home forty-five minutes later, she discovered her husband was also out looking. Upon receiving a message telling her to go to Riddlesworth Hall, Flo went straight away, cycling as fast as she could, and as she approached the Hall, she saw her husband in some bushes and went over to him. There she saw Pat lying in the grass. Blood covered the child's face, her mouth was open and her haunting gaze was fixed skyward. Pat was unconscious. At that time Flo's husband had already sent for a doctor, so he and Flo stayed at the scene until the doctor arrived and the child was taken to hospital.

Lastly, Flo Pask told Garner that she had been the one to formally identify Pat's body as it lay in hospital.

"The body that I saw at Bury St. Edmunds Hospital on Wednesday 6th May, was the body of Patricia Ann Cupit, aged six years and seven months. I have no idea what happened to Patricia. I have always told her not to talk to strangers, but she was not a shy girl."

ALBERT BALLS' STATEMENT

While Mr Pask was being interviewed, Police Constable Woods, also of the Norfolk County Constabulary, visited the young lad who accompanied Mr Pask in the search for Pat, to get his statement. 13-years-old Albert Balls went to the same school as Pat, although his route to school saw him cycle along a road rather than walk the track through the park. He said he never saw her at all that day and after school he went to see Mr Pask about an unrelated matter concerning a message from a blacksmith. When he met Mr Pask, he was asked if he had seen Pat, but he replied he had not, to which Mr Pask replied, "We will go and look for her." The boy confirmed he followed Mr Pask on his cycle, across the park, to visit the school, then back again around Riddlesworth Hall. It was just after passing the Hall that he saw the child's hat lying on the grass.

"It was about 5.45pm when I saw her hat. I cycled past the same spot with Mr Pask, when I came to school with him about 5.30pm, but did not see the hat then. The hat was probably there but I never saw it."

Both he and Mr Pask dropped their cycles to search further, each one taking a different flank around the trees.

"On leaving the school we went back just past the Hall, along the pathway, when I saw Patricia's hat lying on the grass, on the side nearest the Hall about five yards from the path. We left our cycles and searched for her. Mr Pask went to some bushes and I went the other way. Mr Pask came back and went and spoke to a teacher who was playing cricket nearby. They both went across to the bushes again and Mr Pask told me to keep away."

That was as far as Albert could remember. It also confirmed Mr Pask's version of events.

OTHER STATEMENTS

Despite asking for the assistance of London's Metropolitan Police, the Norfolk County Constabulary had not sat back. In fact, they had been actively catching up with people connected to Pat and taking down their statements. At 11.30am, while Mr Pask and Albert Balls were being interviewed, and just over four hours after the girl had died, Inspector George Dye, from Thetford police station, visited the victim's school governess, Ms Samples, to see if there was anything she might be able to offer them in the way of a clue. She painted a picture of the girl's appearance:

"She is six years of age, she was very well kept, very intelligent and bright, of average size for her age, but very dainty, well developed and pretty."

Ms Samples said, because of Pat's friendly nature, she felt it was likely the girl would have stopped and talked to anyone who engaged in conversation with her. She also confirmed she was not overly concerned when Pat hadn't arrived at school on the morning of the 5th May, as it was not unusual for the child to be absent. She confirmed that Mr Pask did indeed visit her at the school that evening, to enquire about the girl. Something that stuck in her head was what Mr Pask said as he left her. She mentioned this in her statement:

"At 5pm, on the 5th May, 1942, Mr Pask, the foster father, came to the school to enquire about Pat and when I told him that the girl had not been to school, he said, well, I must go and look in a ditch for her!"

Perhaps Mr Pask said this out of sheer frustration and worry? Or perhaps he felt the governess should have done more to alert him of Pat's non-attendance? Inspector Dye, upon leaving the school mistress, then made for his next port of call, another 13-years-old lad who saw the girl lying barely-alive in the bushes. Once Pat had been discovered, news travelled fast and John Basil Smith cycled to the scene with his mates to see what was going on. He told the Inspector he saw the victim after Mr Pask had found her. He recognised the coconut matting covering the body as something he and his brother had taken from the grounds of Riddlesworth Hall a couple of years ago. They had laid it in the gorse bushes as a floor for their 'den' but now it had weeds growing through it. It seems the attacker must have grabbed it in haste to cover over his actions.

Dye's day was filled with interviews, spending 15 to 30 minutes at each one. At 12.15pm he interviewed a local man, William Lydle, who reported that a week ago he saw a ginger haired man, lying down on the grass in the park. He said the man had no obvious reason to be there because it was 7.15pm at night. He also noted the man was wearing a soldier's khaki battledress. At the time, Mr Lydle had been accompanied across the park by his brother. Both were walking to attend a Home Guard meeting, coincidentally held at Pat's school. The brothers spoke to the ginger haired man, but they got no response, so continued on their way.

Dye then spoke to another local man, Gordon Anness, who also claimed to have seen the same ginger haired man walking along the same track the child took. However, this sighting was made on Sunday, 3rd May, a couple of days before the attack on Pat. Although no one had seen this ginger-haired man on the day of the attack, it was, nonetheless, a lead.

Another Norfolk policeman, Sergeant Alfred Firman, had also been busy gathering statements. He interviewed 54-years-old Herbert Hardiment, who reckoned he had also seen a man lying down in bushes near Riddlesworth Hall. The soldier appeared to be holding a small pair of binoculars, similar in shape to opera glasses, while scanning the sky, as though he was looking for aircraft. Hardiment said this made him look skyward too but he saw nothing, so he had no idea what the man was looking for. It all seemed very suspicious. Could it be the man was looking toward the Hall, where the school girls were boarding? Perhaps spying on them during their tennis and hockey sessions? Hardiment was herding cattle when he saw the man, so he could not stay to observe further, but he did report his suspicions to his foreman. Hardiment reckoned the man was in his late-20s, maybe 30 years of age, and was about 5-foot 8-inches tall, clean shaven and had ginger hair! In terms of suspects, the ginger-haired man was the main one after the first day of police interviews.

The police had then expanded their efforts to include soldiers billeted at the small army camp on Riddlesworth Park. However, enquiries were very much at an early stage. This camp, housing Royal Engineers and Pioneer Corps servicemen, was nothing more than a few huts that sprung up in the war to accommodate sleeping quarters, latrines and a N.A.A.F.I. hut for the benefit of those billeted there. The N.A.A.F.I. (Navy Army Air Force Institute) provided comfort for servicemen across the world, often in the form of a shop or canteen, and even entertainment. From the camp the servicemen were sent off to work in the countryside and unlike infantry soldiers, their work was about digging, building and dismantling, rather than the tactics of warfare. Thetford Police brought a handful of the servicemen over to their police station to have statements taken. Those who were interviewed seemed innocuous enough, with alibis and names of others who could verify their whereabouts on the day of the attack. However, one man did stand out, a private named James Keeling, who had ginger hair and owned a pair of binoculars. He said in his statement:

"I have a pair of field glasses, and I often go for a walk on the Riddlesworth Park. In fact, I went there yesterday afternoon, 5th May, 1942. I have no special reason for going there, it is just to have a look round. I have no interest in the girls at the Hall, and I use my glasses for looking at birds or planes etc. I have never seen any small girls walking across the park. The only persons I saw yesterday were the girls from the school, and when they came out of their school, I should say, between 2.30pm and 3pm, I came away. I was on my job at the N.A.A.F.I. canteen, Riddlesworth from 7.45am to 11.10am on 5th May 1942, and never left the N.A.A.F.I."

Another soldier, Private James Dormand, claimed to have been on parade at 8am on the morning of the attack. He reckoned there were five others with him and, upon being dismissed, he returned to his bunk to put away his gas mask and equipment. He then walked the short distance to the cookhouse for a cup of tea with another soldier who was nicknamed 'Pompey', then, later that morning, he was transported to Cambridge for a medical assessment. He went to great lengths to prove his innocence, with the soldier emphasising he was a married father of two young children and that five other soldiers would account for his whereabouts on the morning Pat was attacked.

Private Patrick Murphy also found himself inside Thetford police station giving a statement. He was one of the soldiers on parade with the aforementioned Dormand, on the morning Pat was attacked, and confirmed his comrade's version of events. He too went to the N.A.A.F.I. hut, initially to get some cigarettes, but not having any coupons or able to borrow some, he settled for a cup of tea and two buns. Murphy tells Garner he saw new soldiers arrive at the camp that morning, men from the Reconnaissance Company. He stopped for a brief chat before going on his way. He later went around the camp picking up litter and could not say he saw anyone acting suspiciously, but he mentioned he had lost his forage cap, and suspected another soldier of taking it. He named Lance Corporal Gerald Hillary as the culprit, but offered no explanation to why Hillary may have lost his. Like Dormand before him, Murphy also felt compelled to give an insight into his own personal life. He claimed to have a girlfriend back home in Uddingston, Scotland, although he was not married, nor did he have children.

Chief Inspector Barratt can also rely upon the Norfolk

police version of events. Constable Arthur Youngs, stationed at Garboldisham, Norfolk, received a telephone call at 6.20pm on the evening of the attack and immediately went to the scene, arriving 15 minutes later. His account makes for harrowing reading.

"When I arrived, I saw Mr Pask, who was standing where a girl's hat was lying on the ground. The hat was lying loosely on the grass the right way up. Mr Pask took me through the trees and showed me where the child was lying. I then saw Doctor Walton of Hopton and Miss Clarke and Miss Neale from the school. Mrs Pask was also there.

Doctor Walton was kneeling on the right side of the child, about level with her waist. The coconut matting was lying near the child. The child's knees were slightly raised and the feet were about one foot apart. Both her arms were straight by her sides. The child's knickers were still on her legs, and were down to just above her knees. The dress was pulled up, the bottom of the dress being about in line with her navel. The undergarments were also up, exposing the naked body. The child's overcoat was still on but was also unbuttoned and open."

Youngs then said his focus turned from the child, to searching around the body to see if there had been any sign of a struggle, such as leaves disturbed, or blood spots elsewhere. He found nothing. If the child had struggled to escape her attacker, then he saw no evidence of it. Youngs had also carried out another solemn duty that night. One that saw him stay by the side of the child through the night.

"Although the child was unconscious, she groaned and moved her arms and legs very gently when touched. The doctor was unable to give the child any treatment and ordered her removal to hospital. The ambulance arrived at 7pm and she was conveyed to the West Suffolk Hospital at Bury St. Edmunds. I accompanied her in the ambulance.

On arriving there, she was taken to the Children's Ward and placed on a bed in her clothing. I was present when she was undressed at 9pm and took possession of each garment, and shoes, as they were handed to me. I placed each garment, and shoes, in a separate paper. I kept these garments and handed them to Detective Inspector Garner at 11am on 6th May, 1942.

I was present with the child the whole of the time from when she was removed to hospital to when she died at 6.50am on 6th May, 1942. She did not regain consciousness and did not speak."

Youngs may have only been doing his duty, remaining by Pat's side in case she awoke and could offer valuable evidence. Nonetheless, for remaining with her, as her life expired, the 24-years-old showed compassion beyond his years.

TO THE SCENE OF THE CRIME

Chief Inspector Barratt, along with his colleague, Detective Sergeant Webb, has been through a whirlwind since stepping off the train at Thetford. They were only informed of today's posting at 6pm last night, so barely had a few hours to cobble together some clothes and personal belongings. Yet, in the two or three hours since arriving at Thetford they have been quickly brought up to speed on the case. Following a quick lunch, they are again in the police car, but their destination this time takes them out of Thetford. The car, driven by Detective Inspector Garner, travels eastward, with the forest surrounding Thetford giving way to countryside and farmland on either side of the road. The car heads toward Diss, for about 20 minutes, but then turns off the main road and heads down a long drive toward the impressive Riddlesworth Hall. Their destination being the scene of the attack.

The car turns left, driving past the front entrance of Riddlesworth Hall, then leaves the Hall grounds by means of a dirt track that cuts through the trees to take the car on to Riddlesworth Park. The track is nothing more than flattened grass and sand. A few trees and bushes dot the landscape of the 200-acre park, with the car seemingly destined for one clump of trees in particular, known locally as Ladies Grove. At the front of the clump is a 40-foot cedar tree, around it are smaller beech trees and gorse bushes. The car stops near the cedar tree and the men take this as their cue to get out. They are directed by Garner to make their way toward the bushes that grow around the trees.

The men are then shown the exact location where Pat's unconscious body was found lying on the ground. Barratt notes the bushes screen it from the dirt track and the Hall. The ground around lies littered with brown beech leaves, probably fallen from the surrounding trees last autumn. Some of the leaves have been swept aside, most likely by police forensics, to reveal a slight depression of flattened grass growing through the soft sandy soil. This, the men are told, is where the victim's head was located. At about seven-and-a-half inches wide it seems logical. It also represents a sobering silhouette of Pat's head. Another solemn reminder of the crime, are beech leaves within the hollow, which have fragmented under the pressure of her head, some still holding the child's dried blood. Early forensics suggests the blood has seeped into the soil to a depth of two-and-a-half inches. Three feet away from this, more leaves have been swept aside to reveal the earth underneath. Here, there are two smaller, but more distinct, depressions in the ground. They are about a foot apart and two inches deep. Garner assures Barratt that the site was left untouched and guarded by the police until the forensics arrived and photographed the area. However, he also informs Barratt that he had knelt in those same depressions to gauge their origins. He confirms they match an adult of his size and suggests the fully grown person was reaching toward the depression where Pat's head impacted into the ground. Pointing to other leaves around the area, which have not been overly disturbed, Garner suggests this probably indicates there was no struggle. Nor was any blood found beyond where the child's head lay. It seems the child was very quickly overpowered.

Garner tells Barratt that he had noted some coconut matting at the scene. It appeared to have been in the bushes some time because it was badly deteriorated, had weeds growing through it and had become a habitat for insects. One piece had been used to cover the girl's body and there were three other pieces left in the bushes. All the pieces had been removed and sent for forensic analysis, as had the girl's possessions, including her school bag, her woollen hat and gloves. Other than that, and the removal of the child to hospital, the scene had been left untouched and under police guard.

AT THE MORTUARY

Chief Inspector Barratt, having visited the scene of the crime for himself, along with Detective Inspector Garner, returns to the car and is next conveyed 18 miles south to Bury St. Edmunds, in Suffolk. In this busiest of days, the pair's next objective is to see for themselves the victim's injuries, which means a visit to the mortuary of the West Suffolk Hospital. Garner has already seen the victim's body. He was at the hospital when Police Constable Youngs brought Flo Pask to the mortuary to formally identify Pat's body. Garner was also there to take possession of her clothing from Youngs, and saw it labelled, packed and sent for forensic analysis. Barratt is impressed with how thorough Garner has been. Within hours of the child dying, Garner had not only overseen the gathering of forensic evidence, including the police photographer documenting the appalling injuries on Pat's body, he had even stayed throughout the child's post-mortem. For sure, Garner will be a valuable asset when Barratt fully takes over the investigation.

The two detectives arrive at the mortuary and are handed the post-mortem report. It makes for grim reading, which some may be particularly sensitive to. The two detectives are not afforded the opportunity to hide from the dreadful injuries incurred on Pat because they are presented with the child's body in front of them. As part of their investigation, they need to cross reference the report with the physical wounds they see on the little 6-years-old's victim's body.

Before them is the naked body of a well-nourished girl, three-feet ten-inches tall, dark hair, with her face and dark hair covered in dry blood. The blood still has leaf fragments attached. Deep wounds are obvious around the left ear, in fact some of the upper part of the ear appears to have been cut off in the attack. Stab wounds are visible below the jaw, to the left cheek and chin. The men can see the chin wound passes up into the mouth, exiting just in front of the girl's teeth. It is here that the bare bone of the jaw is revealed. These have all the hallmarks of knife wounds, a blade not cleanly and precisely being pushed in and out, but roughly thrusted in and moved about whilst it was in the child's body. There is deep bruising to the left shoulder, face and around both eyes; superficial bruising to the chest and lips and round pressure marks, possibly done by the attacker's finger tips, to both legs. Small marks, likely from the attacker's finger nails, mark both sides of the victim's neck. A ligature mark is also visible across the victim's neck, with a pattern matching her vest, which can only mean the vest was pulled so violently that it left its mark in the skin. Perhaps it indicates the attacker came up behind the victim and pulled her off her feet by violently pulling the child's clothing from behind? The report concludes the victim suffered stabbing, partial strangulation and blunt violence to the left side of her head. Death was a combination of a loss of blood, bringing on shock and a cardiac arrest, and a brain compression and bleed, along with a partial strangulation. The forensic report also states there is no evidence that the child had been sexually interfered with. If there is any saving grace in this report then that sentence was the only comfort anyone will find.

At 5pm that day, with the distressing images of the child still fresh in their minds, detectives Barratt and Garner attend the coroner's inquest. It is a brief hearing to formally confirm the identity of the victim. The coroner then adjourns the inquest until 8th June, by which time he hopes to have seen the full forensics report in order to create a clearer picture of what happened to Pat.

Today has been a very busy day for Barratt, yet he is experienced enough to know his detective work actually begins in earnest tomorrow. As the man leading the investigation into the violent murder of an innocent child, he is the one everyone is looking up to, the man tasked with catching the attacker, but as yet he has no concrete leads.

Diss Express – *Riddlesworth tragedy. The child, whose London home is in Norbury, left the house of her foster parents ... to go to school, which she did not reach.*

Dundee Evening Telegraph – *Stabbed girl in bushes. Scotland Yard men in search. Chief Inspector Barrett and Sergeant Webb of Scotland Yard and officers of the Norfolk Police continued their search.*

Daily Mirror – *Police chief hunts child killer. Yesterday, armed with scythes and rakes, detectives and helpers searched round the spot ... for a weapon.*

With no concrete leads, the police, both local and Metropolitan, are no nearer to catching the attacker than they were on the day Pat was attacked. However, with so many soldiers billeted in and around Riddlesworth Park, Chief Inspector Barratt is keen to bring more of them into the investigation. It seems some of the local residents view the soldiers with suspicion. There are certain 'out of bounds' areas for soldiers, such as the grounds of Riddlesworth Hall, yet now and again they are seen either loitering or walking across the playing field. Locals have also had their bicycles and river punts 'borrowed' by soldiers who decide to explore the area on them. The soldiers are transient, here one day and gone the next, perhaps meaning they feel less accountable for any disruption they may cause. Children have been warned to avoid contact with the soldiers, as who knows if there are any 'wrong uns' among them. Today, the day after Barratt's arrival, the police concentrate their efforts on speaking to soldiers from the Pioneer Corps who are billeted at the army camp on the park. The one thing the police are sure about, is that Pat was attacked on her way to school, putting the incident between 7.45am and 8.20am.

The police first speak to Lieutenant Taylor, the commanding officer of the soldiers billeted on Riddlesworth Park. He is not able to offer anything much, other than saying he came across one of his men, Private Robert Kirkpatrick, talking to some workmen on a road outside the camp. He asked the private what he was doing, to which the reply came back:

"Salvaging, sir."

– salvaging being a term for going around camp picking up rubbish or anything else left lying around by the soldiers. The lieutenant spoke abruptly to his man,

"Well, get on with your work."

After this sharp exchange, the lieutenant returned to his office and that was all he could offer to the investigation.

The camp's Colour Sergeant Major, Thomas Gregory, is more forthcoming. He tells the police, that on the day the child was murdered, five servicemen, all privates, were due to be taken to Cambridge to see a medical specialist. It seems those men had been suffering from varying illnesses for some considerable time. At 8am that morning, Gregory got the men – Patrick Murphy, James Dormand, Robert Allen, John Worthy and Robert Kirkpatrick; along with Lance Corporal Frank Allen; to parade in full kit. Whilst on parade he informed them that they were to be picked up by truck and taken to Thetford railway station, where a train would convey them to Cambridge. After about 15 minutes, he dismissed the men and ordered them to walk around the camp picking up litter until their truck arrived. Apparently, a cycle had been stolen from the camp, so they were to keep their eyes open for any signs of that. He also ordered them to collect their haversack rations from the N.A.A.F.I. hut before going on salvage and they were to return for parade at 11am, just as their transport was due to collect them. Gregory reckons none of the men had reported the loss of any of their equipment, such as a knife or bayonet, although one of them, Private Murphy, did admit to having lost his forage cap.

It's fair to say the soldiers on Riddlesworth Park do not offer the impression of being a tight-knit unit. It seems many of them do not know each other too well, nor have much intention of interacting socially. They come from varied backgrounds, some married, some single, there are English and Scottish, some happy to be there, others more reluctant. In fact, in many ways, they are as much strangers to each other as they are to the local community.

Next up to be questioned is Lance Corporal Frank Allen, who has served with the Pioneer Corp for 10 months. He confirms he and the other five men were on parade, in front of CSM Gregory, at 8am on the day Pat was attacked, but also adds that Private Murphy arrived late for the 11am parade, with Murphy announcing he had lost his hat and had to borrow one. Allen also claims Murphy was the only one not wearing his battledress on parade, but instead was sporting an army overcoat. Allen also thought he saw one of the men – perhaps Murphy, but it could have equally been Worthy, he was not sure which – walking around the camp at some time around 10am, just before the soldiers collected their rations. Murphy, he claims, was the only one who did not collect his rations before going to Cambridge. The five men then left the camp, as planned, and he could not recall anything exceptional about any of their behaviour. Other than that, Allen tells the police, there was nothing else out of the ordinary that morning.

Another soldier with something to say about Murphy's missing cap is Private Alfred Hyde. He had come to the camp with two forage caps – one that had shrunk over time, which he wore while working; while the other was a more pristine example and kept for when he wanted to look good. The shrunken cap had been missing for a couple of weeks, but then one day Murphy came up to him and said, "Here's your cap." Hyde admits this was strange because he did not believe Murphy had taken the cap, so perhaps the soldier had simply found it and was returning it. If that was the case, Hyde queries, then why had Murphy not kept the cap for himself? Especially as Murphy had previously informed Hyde he had lost his own cap. Perhaps Murphy was simply being honest.

The attention of the police then turns to the five privates who had been sent to Cambridge. James Dormand and Patrick Murphy had already been interviewed at Thetford Police Station on 6th May, but their statements offered little. Today, John Worthy and Robert Allen have nothing much to offer either, other than to confirm they were on parade at 8am and had never seen the girl during their time at the camp. Robert Kirkpatrick confirms he stopped his litter pick to speak to some workmen on the road by the camp, he also confirms his commanding officer, Lieutenant Taylor, spoke to him, but he cannot recall exactly what the lieutenant said to him. He then removed all the litter he had collected and sought refuge in the Sergeants' Mess, where he went for a cup of tea.

All things considered, speaking with the soldiers in the camp today has not borne much for the police, although Barratt notes the saga of the forage cap has been mentioned a lot. In fact, to a large extent, the investigation so far seems to have been a waste of time. Even the civilians working in the camp's N.A.A.F.I. have been unable to offer much other than seeing a drunk on a cycle the night before the attack. A wider appeal for anyone travelling near the area has brought a lukewarm response from people living in and around Thetford. Apart from claims of seeing soldiers wearing blue shorts and standing around the area, with one person identifying an Austin 7 parked up nearby, the appeal has brought nothing concrete. Nonetheless, those seemingly unproductive statements are noted, just in case. Away from the camp, there are still leads to be explored at the school, so this is where the police go next.

INTERVIEWS

Mary Eleanor Clarke has been headmistress of the Felixstowe College for Girls since 1929. Prior to that, the 59-years-old had been a teacher in her home county of Hampshire. Following the outbreak of war, and with the real threat of a German attack along the Suffolk coast, the authorities re-located the Felixstowe College for Girls, including 26 staff and ninety-three students, temporarily inland to the luxurious setting of Riddlesworth Hall. The pupils may well be there for the same reason that Pat was housed with the Pasks, but the boarding school girls are far more privileged than the little girl from London. Perhaps they have looked out through their windows and seen Pat walking past in all weathers to attend her tiny community school? Paradoxically, the slaying of little Pat near their hall, has now seen the perceived threat from an enemy attack diminish compared to that of a home-grown one. Upon coming to Riddlesworth, Ms Clarke has taken a couple of rooms on the first floor of the hall, on the western side, namely a bedroom and a dressing room. Two of her windows overlook the dirt track that runs through Riddlesworth Park, so for the police she could be a key witness, more so because she was, along with Albert Pask, one of the first to arrive on the scene. Detective

Inspector Garner meets up with her at Riddlesworth Hall to ask her questions and take her written statement.

Ms Clarke, by her own admission, probably had the best view of the scene, but she tells Garner she saw nothing, despite being in her room that morning between 7.45am and 8.30am. Nor did she hear anyone scream and she was certain she would have heard one, if it had been made during that time. She had been busy getting ready for the school's morning assembly of prayers, usually held in the drawing room, so she was not stood staring out the window. Nonetheless, while she was in her room and catching the occasional glimpse out, she saw nothing out of the ordinary. She recalls that some of her junior pupils, housed in nearby Garboldisham, were 20 minutes late that morning on account of their bus being delayed, but upon their arrival all pupils and staff were accounted for and attended the school assembly. Ms Clarke also tells Garner that the grounds of Riddlesworth Hall had been made out of bounds to all soldiers. Indeed, she had hardly ever seen any soldiers in the vicinity unless they were on manoeuvres. However, this arrangement had become lax recently and she has seen one or two walking nearby. Some have even taken to walking through the grounds as a short cut.

The headmistress reflects upon the events of the evening of the attack. She confirms her sports mistress,

Beatrice Neale, came to her as she sat in her study to explain that a man had rushed past the girls who were playing tennis. He then approached Miss Neale in a distressed manner, shouting, "There's a child murdered in the bushes and she's crying." Ms Clarke followed the sports teacher out of the study to meet Albert Pask at the main entrance to the Hall. He begged the headmistress to come with him, so she followed to the scene of the attack. By the time she got there, there was already a small group of boys gathering to observe, and upon entering the bushes she saw the child's body covered by the matting. Once the matting was pulled down, it was obvious the girl had been attacked. A horrific wound behind the girl's ear had led to significant blood loss, which upon drying had caused leaves to stick to the side of the child's face. Ms Clarke states she was also at the scene when the doctor arrived twenty minutes later and she suggests the child exhibited clear signs she was in pain when the doctor examined her. The girl's head however did not move, nor did her eyes deviate from an upward stare, thus indicating the girl's condition was very serious.

"I remained there until the ambulance took her away. I could not say whether she had a hair slide or not. Her handbag was lying on her left beyond her reach. One of her gloves was beside her with the fingers inside out. We found the other one

when her body was lifted on to the stretcher, it had been beneath her."

Detective Inspector Garner asks the headmistress if she has had any experiences, bad or otherwise, with the soldiers billeted in the park.

"The precincts of the Hall were put out of bounds to the first lot of troops occupying the camp and at one time we seldom saw a soldier near the Hall unless they were on manoeuvres. We noticed a greater laxity just a few days prior to the tragedy, and I have seen soldiers singly, or in twos or greater numbers, using the drive or walking by the rivers. I have also seen soldiers using the punt which is kept in the boathouse down by the river.

At the time the ambulance came, there was a whole group of soldiers passing by, and two of them dropped behind the others, one dark and one fair. The dark one was aged about 20, of medium height, proportionate build. I think his hair was on the long side. He stooped down to tie up his shoe and had a good look round. I don't think he was wearing a cap."

SATURDAY, 9TH MAY, 1942

Sunderland Daily Echo & Shipping Gazette – *Darling of village. Child victim of slayer. None of our children is safe while the fiend is at large.*

Liverpool Evening Express – *Village seeks*

vengeance. Chief Inspector Barratt and his assistant, Detective-Sergeant Webb, who was also engaged in the "Babes in the Wood" inquiry in East Anglia, left their headquarters at Thetford to revisit the scene.

Croydon Times – *Norbury Girl Evacuee Murdered. Marks on the child's throat indicated that an attempt had been made to strangle her. There were also signs of interference.*

Daily Mirror – *Call by mother of murdered girl. "Please tell all mothers who read of my little Pat that they must not be afraid." Mrs Cupit, mother of six-year-old evacuee Pat Cupit who was found stabbed in the throat at Riddlesworth, Norfolk, said this to the Daily Mirror last night. "Tell them to keep the children in the country, where children belong," she added.*

Detective Inspector Garner returns to Riddlesworth Hall on Saturday, 9th May to speak with the school's sports mistress, Beatrice Neale, known to her colleagues as 'Betty'. She tells the detective that her day was no different to any other, that is until about 5.40pm. She had gone to the cricket nets with a few senior girls, then sometime later a man, who she now knows to be Albert Pask, came running across the field shouting something incoherently. As he got nearer, she understood Albert was saying something about a girl lying in the bushes and he was asking her to go back there with him. She asked him if he knew the girl, to which he acknowledged he did. He appeared very distressed, thus making her believe his story and so she went with him to the scene of the attack. When they got there, she saw Pat lying on the ground in bushes, partially covered by matting. Albert said:

"Don't touch her!"

He then asked Ms Neale to fetch for a doctor and the police. The teacher's statement then paints a scene of the staff at the Hall becoming embroiled in the chaotic aftermath of the discovery of Pat's body.

"I left him a little way from the scene to do this and as I did so another mistress, Miss Hoskins, arrived on the scene. I noticed three or four small boys standing nearby. I went straight to the office and told Miss Stacey, who 'phoned the doctor and the police. I also informed Miss Clarke. I went back to the scene and met Mr Pask and his wife at the front door. Miss Clarke, myself, Mr Pask and his wife returned to the scene. I stayed with the child, with Mrs Pask, for about half an hour until the doctor arrived."

Ms Neale reckons that in the minutes before the doctor arrived, Pat frequently tried to lift her right arm and draw her knees up, but the pain when doing so appeared to be too much so she instead groaned in agony. The teacher also says the child, labouring in her breathing, made a gurgling noise in her throat, to which she assumes indicates some form of internal bleeding. She tells Garner that when the doctor arrived, she left the scene and made her way back to the hall, stopping only once to direct a policeman to where Pat lay. She can offer nothing in the way of leads into who may have carried out the attack and she saw nothing out of the ordinary during that day.

"*I cannot remember seeing any soldiers near the Hall in the morning and I cannot remember seeing any singly in the afternoon, but I have seen them in the drive leading to the road, mostly in the evening, talking to the maids. The only people I have ever noticed come across the park, apart from the soldiers, are Mr Tortice, our groundsman, and the village school children, including the dead child.*"

She is one of the few people who remembers seeing Pat walking along the dirt track to school, sometimes alone, sometimes accompanied by Flo Pask. She also mentions Mr Tortice, caretaker at Riddlesworth Hall, who is now of interest to Garner. He sends Inspector George Dye, of the Norfolk County Constabulary, to pay the man a visit.

Arthur Tortice lives in a cottage just a few hundred yards from the Pasks, although he moved there only recently. The cottage is on the track previously walked by Pat to school and is about a 10-minute walk from the scene of the attack. In fact, Arthur tells Inspector George Dye, he walks along the same track himself to work every morning, but cannot recall ever seeing the girl. On the day in question, Tortice says he arrived at Riddlesworth Hall at 8am, with his first task being to get the main boiler up and running. He then got wood in for the fireplaces to heat the building and attended to a couple of motor cars belonging to the Hall. He had planned to cut the lawns at 10.30am, but the lawn mower was being repaired, so instead he did other chores before cutting the grass later that afternoon. He neither saw any commotion beyond the grounds or anyone acting suspiciously near them. As an eyewitness, Arthur offers nothing.

Whilst it may appear the police are not achieving much, the Riddlesworth Hall headmistress, Ms Clarke, while not offering much assistance in the apprehension of a suspect, did say something that would later prove poignant. In her statement she noted this about the victim:

"… I think that if she had screamed when I was in the room, I should have heard her."

Perhaps this evidence indicated the girl was taken by surprise? Or did it signify something more sinister? Perhaps the girl knew her attacker and gladly went with them? The police know that most murderers are known to their victims. Detective Garner's next visit is to Edwin Curson, and his son Ralph, who are both colleagues of Albert Pask.

Edwin Curson lives at Rosemary Cottage, Knettishall, which is just over half a mile, as the crow flies, from the scene of the attack. The 48-years-old farm steward at Hall Farm, Knettishall, tells Garner he gets to work at 7.30am every day, and his first task is always to allocate duties to all the employees on the farm, including Albert Pask, who is employed as a tractor driver. On the day in question, Albert arrived at work on time, also at 7.30am, and was given the task of bush harrowing, which involves dragging a large rake behind the tractor with the purpose of levelling off the ground. This was on a field about 500 yards south of the attack on Pat, but it was also the other side of the Little Ouse River. Edwin says Albert was there until just before lunch time, about 12.15pm, and apart from the last hour when his son, Ralph, joined him, he says Albert worked alone in the field. Garner presses him about Mr Pask's movements that day. Edwin is sure he did not deviate from the task of bush harrowing because, although he did not observe the man himself, he did hear Albert's tractor working incessantly over the field without stopping. He was sure, with the amount of work he put in, there was no opportunity for the man to stop. Even if he had stopped, he would have had to either cross the river by foot or come over one of two bridges, both of which passed by Curson's home, so Albert would have been seen if he had left the field he was working in. In the afternoon, Albert worked in the yard, alongside nine other farm workers, including Ralph, until 5pm, so he reckoned there was no way the man could have been involved in Pat's murder. To back this up, Edwin tells Garner he has known Albert since the man left school and came to work on the farm. Albert, he says, is a reliable and sober man, who is happily married and incapable of hurting anyone.

Garner then asks to speak to Edwin's son, Ralph, who lives with his father, mother and 11-years-old brother. Ralph confirms he too started work at 7.30am that day and saw Albert Pask already there at that time. He also confirms he went to assist him just before lunch to pack up and bring the bush harrowing equipment back to the yard. It seems Albert then had lunch in the stable and worked in the yard all afternoon before leaving at 5pm. Other than that, the 16-years-old lad can offer nothing else about Albert's movements. However, the Cursons' statements do seem to put him in the clear.

DOCTOR WALTON

While Detective Inspector Garner is visiting Betty Neale

at the school, Chief Inspector Barratt visits the doctor who arrived at the scene of the attack. Doctor Henry Beckles Gall Walton lives at Hopton House, in the village of Hopton, about four miles from Riddlesworth Hall. He is 69-years-old and a veteran of the Great War, having served as a Lieutenant-Colonel in the Royal Army Medical Corps from 1914. During his military career he was also stationed in South Africa and India before his retirement from the army in 1921. He may have attended many wounded men on numerous battlefields, but an attack on a child just a few miles from his home was something else. The doctor confirms to Barratt that he did indeed receive a telephone call from Riddlesworth Hall about a child found lying in bushes, which was about 6pm on the evening of the attack. He says he immediately jumped into his car and left home, arriving about half-an-hour later. Barratt asks many questions about what the doctor saw, he then makes notes while the doctor replies. With the conclusion of the meeting, Barratt reads his notes out aloud to the doctor. The notes will form the basis of the doctor's statement, so he asks the doctor to confirm they truly reflect the doctor's version of events. The doctor agrees they do. Barratt will then face the arduous task of typing this all up once he returns to Thetford police station, to then return to Dr Walton and ask him to sign this formal version. The doctor's statement is replicated here, word for word, with all its stark detail laid bare.

"*At about 6pm on the 5th May, 1942, I received a telephone call from Riddlesworth Hall that a child had been found in the grounds of the Park, severely injured, and asking me to go at once. I went there by car, arriving about 6.20pm to 6.30pm. I was shown the place where the child was lying. I saw the child lying on her back, head to north, feet to south, arms by her side. There was no voluntary movement, but the child was alive and sufficiently conscious to resent being disturbed. She was fully dressed, except for her hat. Her coat was unbuttoned and had fallen open, her dress and petticoat were all pulled up and her knickers drawn down her thighs to her knees. The lower part of her abdomen and private parts were exposed. Faecal matter was on her knickers, and also stained the inner surface of the thighs. There was no evidence of seminal discharge or that the vaginal passages had been penetrated by the male organ.*

The face, hair and neck of the child was matted with blood which was congealed. There was no actual bleeding when I saw the child. There was a stab wound about 1" on the left side from the symphys (sic) of the jaw, the wound was about 1" x ¾" tapering upwards and inwards to the floor of the mouth. Air appeared to be escaping from this wound. The tongue was blue and had fallen back into the pharynx. There were two other apparent stab wounds, one on the right of the chin and one on the left cheek.

The head was in a recess in the ground and falling back away from the throat showing bruising of the lower part of the neck, one mark about ¼" wide extending round the front of the neck, which appeared to have been done by a cord which marked the flesh intermittently. The mark above this mark appeared to have been made by the pressure of the forefinger and thumb, the thumb being to the right of the windpipe.

She appeared to have bled from the nose, the left eyelid was swollen and oedematous, so that it was with difficulty that the lid was opened and the eye examined. This appeared to have been caused by a blow, possibly with a fist. The eye ball was normal but squinted slightly to the left. The right eye squinted inwards.

The condition of the girl was very serious and I ordered her immediate removal to hospital, which was done by Thetford Ambulance.

This statement has been read to me and is true.

(Signed) Henry B.G. Walton.

Statement taken and written by Chief Inspector Barratt, C.O., C.1., on the 9th May, 1942."

SUNDAY 10TH MAY, 1942

Sunday Post – *Girl Evacuee Murdered. Home Guards, police, and villagers ranged over a wide area of farms and parkland in the heart of Norfolk last night in search of the murderer of Pat Ann Cupit, 6½-year-old Norbury evacuee.*

The People – *Villagers fiend hunt. The ground has been searched without result by villagers, Home Guards and police for the weapon with which the child was stabbed in the throat.*

Sunday Mirror – *His vow of vengeance. Before he left this tiny Norfolk village for his home in London today, an RAF sergeant, tragic father of six-year-old Pat Ann Cupit, who was brutally murdered in a lonely wood here, took a solemn oath of vengeance.*

Yesterday the Daily Mirror printed quotes from Anne Cupit, Pat's mother. Today, the Sunday edition, has printed what Leonard had to say when their reporter caught up with him at Riddlesworth, just before he was due to return to London. The newspaper does not disguise the raw emotion in his words.

"I have been walking through the countryside, where my little girl was so happy, with a grim hope in my heart. Patsy was so happy here in this village, playing among the flowers and sunshine.

I have been hoping that God would allow me to meet this killer face to face. If I meet him, Heaven help him. I will give him far worse than he gave my little Pat. There will be no trial and no hanging, for I will kill him, and so avenge my little girl.

If this killer does not hang, I will kill him with my own hands."

men stationed there. Conditions are far from luxurious. Surprisingly, these small huts house almost 350 m████████ of them from the 218th Company, Pioneer Corps, along with a contingent of the 1st Reconnaissance Regiment, with the latter arriving on the afternoon before the attack. In addition to these units, soldiers from the Royal Engineers, billeted elsewhere, occasionally frequent the camp, as do civilian electricians, labourers and canteen workers. With no proper security fencing, just a slight wooden fence, it seems anyone can come and go as they please. At the northern end of the camp are the latrines.

Chief Inspector Barratt and his New Scotland Yard colleague, Detective Sergeant Webb, are among those visiting the army camp, but once again initial investigations reveal nothing out of the ordinary. However, that changes when they speak to Corporal Edward John Molson, who offers them the insight they have longed for. Molson had been at the camp for a month, but was subsequently reassigned elsewhere the day after the attack, therefore he has had no contact with the police up to now. Molson tells the two detectives that on 5th May, at 7.45 am, he paraded with others and was tasked with taking a team of soldiers to remove a tarpaulin cover from a disused ammunition dump, at the southern tip of the army camp, which is just behind the outbuildings of Mr Tortice's cottage. For this, he assigned privates James Wyeth, John Morgan and Albert ███████ridge to go to the dump. Two other privates, Morris and Little, were assigned a job of excavating a trench so a water pipe could be connected to the back of the N.A.A.F.I. canteen. It was just after 8am that the team collected tools for their tasks ahead and Corporal Molson led them out. Their first stop was to leave the two at the trench. Molson ensured they knew what they had to do and then proceeded with the three others to the ammunition dump, about 200 yards away. Molson stayed with the group at the dump, roughly between 8.15am and 8.30am. Interestingly, the spot was just 100 yards from the dirt track where Pat would have walked, and at about the time she would have done so on the day she was attacked. Perhaps Molson had seen the girl that morning? Sadly, he told Barratt he did not see her, in fact from where the group was working, he reckons the track was partially obscured by Mr Tortice's cottage and tree foliage. Molson was also certain none of the three men left the ammunition dump during the time he was there.

At 8.30am, Molson informed the group he was going back to check up on the other two men working the trench and that he would return soon. It was at this time that one of the men, Private Wyeth, sought permission to go to the latrines at the other end of the camp, for which Molson authorised. Molson then went to visit the other two men, found them hard at work and stayed with them for about half-an-hour. After this time, he returned to the ▮▮▮▮ at the ammunition dump. To his surprise there were only two men working because Private Wyeth had still not returned. It was, at most, a five-minute walk to the latrines and back. He turned and looked down the track toward the latrines and saw Wyeth walking toward them. When Wyeth got to the group, he appeared red-faced, leading the men to enquire about what he had been up to.

"I said to him, 'Where the hell have you been?' and he said, 'For a shit.'

I said, 'What are you sweating for?' and he said, 'It's the bloody weather. Don't you think it's hot?' Or words to that effect. I said, 'Well now, let's get some bloody work done.'

Apart from his hot condition there was nothing else I noticed wrong, but I had no occasion to further examine him. I estimate he was away from his work from 8.30am to about 9.10am."

Private Morgan also had reason to leave the ammunition dump, on account of cutting his hand on a hatchet. Molson sent him to the sick bay to get it dressed, but the soldier was only gone a few minutes. Molson alternated his time between the men in the trench and those at the dump, finding both parties working hard when he arrived. This led him to think none of the men, apart from Wyeth and Morgan, left their work stations th█████rning.

Privates Wyeth and Morgan are now of interest to Barratt and Webb, so it is imperative they speak with those soldiers next. Private John Morgan, a Scotsman, tells Barratt he had joined the Pioneer Corps just last month and was sent to the camp three weeks before the attack on the girl. He confirms that on the day of the incident he had been sent to dismantle the ammunition dump and that Corporal Molson led the group. Morgan recalls that at about 8.30am, Private Wyeth asked Molson to be excused to go to the latrine, a request Molson granted, but Morgan did not see which way Wyeth went. Even though the latrines were just a minute or two walk away, Wyeth was gone at least half-an-hour and only re-appeared after Corporal Molson had returned from inspecting the lads working in the trench. Morgan also recalls that Wyeth was red faced and sweating when he returned. He also heard the conversation between Molson and Wyeth.

"Wyeth had not returned and Molson asked where he was. Two or three minutes later I saw Wyeth coming from the direction of the N.A.A.F.I. When he reached us, Molson said, 'Where have you been?'

Wyeth said he had been to the lavatory, but I do not

remember his exact words. Wyeth looked very hot and was sweating. I said to him, 'What are you sweating for?' and he said 'It's the heat. I've been walking down the road.'

I said, "It looks as if you have been running or using a pick and shovel."

Other than that, Morgan had not noticed anything suspicious that day, nor had he ever seen the girl walk past. He confirms Molson's statement that the tree foliage obscured the view of the pathway. The detectives ask Morgan if Wyeth had been carrying a bayonet when he returned, but the soldier replied that he had not seen one.

Barratt is now intrigued as to where Private Wyeth went during the time he left the ammunition dump, and why he had returned hot and sweating. He finds the soldier and speaks to him about this. Wyeth, like Morgan, had joined the camp at Riddlesworth just three weeks prior to the attack. The 5th May saw him on work detail at Riddlesworth Park for the first time. In fact, on that day, Wyeth and three other lads had boarded a truck to be taken to Southwood Camp, just four miles away at Snarehill, on the outskirts of Thetford, but Corporal Molson arrived and, in no uncertain terms, told them to get off because they were going to take down a cover on an ammunition dump at the Riddlesworth Camp. Wyeth admits he needed the toilet whilst working there and that Corporal Molson gave him permission to leave his work station. He also admits he made a diversion along the way, saying it was to visit his hut and grab a newspaper to take to the latrines. As he came out of his hut, he saw Private Morgan going in and the two men had a brief discussion.

"When I came out of my hut, I saw Morgan coming up towards my hut. He said, 'Where are you going?' and I said 'I'm going to the lavatory.'

I asked him where he was going and he said, 'I'm going for some tools.' I then went to the lavatory near the main road, near the Guard Room. I sat on the lavatory for about half an hour reading the paper. I think it was the Daily Mirror. I did not see anyone in the lavatory that I knew, and I did not see the lavatory cleaner. When I left the lavatory, I walked straight back towards the dump where I was working, using the little path through the camp.

After I had passed the N.A.A.F.I. canteen I saw the Corporal walking in front of me towards the dump. When he saw me coming, he said, 'You've been a long time, what about some work being done?' I told him I had been to the lavatory and had been reading a paper on the lavatory seat. One of the Privates, I think it was Woodbridge, asked me what I was sweating for. I said, 'It's a close morning'. I sweat very freely, and was wearing a battle dress with a denim suit on top."

Wyeth then suggests he remained working at the ammunition dump until lunchtime, after which he joined the rest of the team in the N.A.A.F.I. canteen. He confirms that, just like the other men, he had not seen the girl walk past, nor had he seen anyone acting suspiciously that day. Barratt and Garner then return to Private Morgan for clarification on one of Wyeth's comments. Morgan says in his next statement:

"I should have mentioned that sometime during the morning – I am not sure when – I was sent by Molson to his hut for a pair of pliers. I do not remember seeing Wyeth or speaking to him whilst I was on this errand. Wyeth used the same hut as Molson."

MONDAY 11ᵀᴴ MAY, 1942

Bradford Observer – *Evacuee murder search. On fresh information, Chief Inspector T. Barrett, of Scotland Yard, and other officers, visited an empty secluded house on the riverside, a mile from where Pat was found. The river may be dragged.*

Nottingham Evening Post – *Murdered Schoolgirl. Clothing to be examined in Nottingham. The clothing of Pat Ann Cupit … has been sent to Forensic Science Laboratory, Nottingham, for examination. It is hoped that the examination will provide clues which will help in tracing the assailant of the murdered girl*

Daily Mirror – *Rector appeals to parish: "Get*

Chief Inspector Barratt and Detective Sergeant Webb return to the army camp to commence their fourth full day of interviews. Today, they meet someone who claims to have seen Pat walking to school along the track. Private William Crasswell, of the 218th Company, Pioneer Corps, tells Webb that he recalls seeing her, he estimates a fortnight before she was attacked, on the back of a cycle being ridden by a woman. This woman was probably Flo Pask taking Pat to school. However, this was the only time Crasswell saw the girl, so it adds little to the investigation. With reference to what he was doing on the day of the girl's murder, he claims to have been cleaning an 8-cwt truck when he was summoned, along with another soldier, to take a ride on the truck to Thetford to collect coal and bring his own truck back from the repair shop. He says he was in the yard from about 9.15am for about an hour, and then left for Thetford. At no point did he see anyone else in the yard during that time. Two corporals are also questioned, but neither of them can offer anything substantial.

Two civilians working in the N.A.A.F.I. are

interviewed. One mentions Private James Keeling as being a regular in the canteen and it appears the soldier did disappear for part of the morning of the 5th May, however the other N.A.A.F.I. civilian gives Keeling a cast iron alibi, while also claiming the soldier is a decent person. This is the same Keeling who the police interviewed a few days ago because he was identified as being the ginger-haired soldier with binoculars. Once again, they question him about his movements that day, and it is the first time they return to interview someone already spoken to. Keeling tells Barratt, he was cleaning the N.A.A.F.I. canteen on the morning of Tuesday, 5th May. His statement also reads:

"I have mentioned in my previous statement that I have been in the habit of going across the park in the afternoons during my break from canteen work and carrying field glasses with me. The only reason I carry them is to look at the view or birds or aeroplanes. I have no other reason for carrying them and have never been there using them when the girls have been playing tennis.

On Tuesday, the 5th May, 1942, between two and three, I walked across the Park with my glasses and was sitting down near a football field under a tree when I saw the girls from the school come out to play tennis. I immediately left the district and came back to camp. I had only been there a quarter of an hour.

I have been over there four or five times before but usually got back to the camp before five. I have never seen a little girl walking across the park, and so far as I know, I have never seen the little girl who was murdered."

Keeling's second statement matches his first, and offers little in the way of anything new. Yet, he is now on the police radar, especially considering a carpenter employed at Riddlesworth Hall has come forward today to alert the police to a soldier with "light ginger bushy hair" loitering around bushes nearby. However, that sighting bears little relevance to the day of the attack because it goes back a number of days before. Nonetheless, the ginger haired man is standing out, for one reason or another, with locals.

Late that night, two troopers, serving with the 1st Regiment, Reconnaissance Corps, pop into Thetford police station, to drop off a khaki tunic they found lying unattended in the woods near the attack. They are not sure how long it had been there, nor if it bears any significance to the investigation but feel they should hand it in, just in case. Inspector Dye, of Norfolk Constabulary, is on hand to take down their brief statements. Apart from that, this is the sum total from soldiers billeted at the army camp today.

While Barratt and Webb are on the army camp, police

at Thetford receive a visit from a Riddlesworth gamekeeper, Edgar Scillitoe. He has popped in to report a shocking incident he witnessed two nights previous. While he was in the Swan pub, in Garboldisham, a group of soldiers from the Riddlesworth Camp popped in for a drink. One of the men, with reference to the attack on the child, said, "It took me three fucking weeks to plan a bloody murder!" Scillitoe did say the soldier was probably drunk at the time, but felt it worth mentioning to the police nonetheless. Police Constable Edward Gaskin writes the man's statement in his notebook and saves it for the attention of the New Scotland Yard detectives.

Despite so many seemingly dead ends, there is one very poignant interview being conducted on Monday, although not at Riddlesworth, nor at Thetford Police Station, indeed not even in East Anglia. It is conducted in London, at Norbury Police Station. Detective Inspector James Callaghan speaks with Pat's father, Leonard Cupit, who is a sergeant serving in the Royal Air Force. The interview is not because Leonard is a suspect, nor to gain any eye witness account, but instead to gain some background information to Pat's life before the attack. Aged only 6-years-old, her opportunities at having life experiences had been cruelly taken from her, but Leonard tells Callaghan her story the best he can. He speaks about Pat's movements during the war, and tells the detective his daughter was very happy staying with the Pasks and he had managed to visit her five weeks before the attack. As far as he was concerned no one had reason to harm the child. Leonard says, he and his wife consider themselves to have no enemies who would have had cause to attack their daughter. Her loss has left a hole in their family, with no rhyme nor reason as to why she had been targeted in such an horrific way. This heartbreak is not made any easier by the forensic report now being released on the same day that Leonard is interviewed.

WEST MIDLAND FORENSIC SCIENCE LABORATORY

On Monday, 11th May, 1942, James Webster, the director of the West Midland Forensic Science Laboratory, based in Birmingham, releases his forensic report about Pat's demise. The report is essentially in two parts – the post-mortem and an assessment, based upon forensic science, of how he believes the child met her violent end. He sends the report directly to Detective Inspector Garner, of the Norfolk County Constabulary. Webster also acknowledges receipt of more evidence, namely the child's clothing, which he had collected from Birmingham's New Street Police Station on Saturday 9th May.

Webster's autopsy, conducted at 3.45pm, on Wednesday 6th May, took place at the West Suffolk Hospital Mortuary, Bury St. Edmunds, just nine hours after Pat died. It notes the state of the child's body before it was cleaned – naked; all clothing having been removed and sent for forensic testing. Upon cleaning the body, stab wounds to the face, hair and neck, were revealed, with bruising to both eyes, the face, lips, neck and shoulders also apparent. The front of the neck displays abrasions, perhaps pressure marks left from someone else's fingers. Both eyes are swollen and show signs of haemorrhaging. The internal examination reveals the child as being very healthy, with the only issue Webster finding is that of a deficiency of blood, which is no surprise as the child lost a lot of it after the attack. It seems, with a lack of blood, the heart struggled to pump its vital fluid around the body, especially to the lungs, which are pale and anaemic. The bruising on the child's neck and left shoulder went deep down into the tissue and muscle. It is obvious the child was subjected to a frenzied attack. Webster suggests it was perhaps inflicted by someone suffering a psychosis. None of this is news to Garner, after all he had accompanied Chief Inspector Barratt to the mortuary in the afternoon when the latter arrived at Thetford. He is keen to read the rest of the report, the part where forensics offer a different angle to his investigation. He continues reading.

The report goes on to suggest what might have happened during the attack. The mark around Pat's neck, could be as a result of the attacker grabbing her by the back of the clothing around her neck. Perhaps so violently it lifted the girl from the ground. If so, it would have contributed to her strangulation, perhaps even stifling any attempt at a scream. The child may not have even been aware of the impending attack, especially if the attacker came up quickly behind her. This version of events, however violent it seems, is perhaps better than the thought that Pat knew what was coming and tried to run away, with her attacker reaching out to grab her clothing. There was a chance the marks could have occurred if the attacker dragged the child by her clothing into the bushes to conceal her body, but there was no evidence of the leaves on the ground being disturbed. Webster also concurs the evidence of strangulation was also likely due to when the child was roughly manhandled, and it was unlikely the attacker purposely tried to strangle the child.

Webster goes on to suggest the attacker was not disturbed during the attack, which he concludes took place at approximately 8.30am on the 5th May. Whoever attacked Pat had enough time to pull down her knickers and, although she was not interfered with, had enough time to find some cocoa matting and cover her body up. An alternative scenario is one where the attacker was disturbed and returned later that afternoon to cover the body. Webster also uses his forensic experience to reflect upon how the body was covered, but not the face, and how it may relate to the attacker.

"In my experience of murder cases, where attempts have been made to conceal the body, it has always struck me as something more than coincidental that, when such covering is attempted, if the assailant and the assailed were known to each other, the coverings were more secure and perfect over the murdered person's face than the rest of the body. Whereas *in the case of a stranger committing the murder, the face has not infrequently been left uncovered and the endeavours at concealment confined to the body and legs. Various psychological reasons have been put forward for this, and, whilst I do not set any great store by this observation, it might weigh with other considerations during the investigation as a pointer to whether this child was murdered by a stranger or someone well known to her."*

If Webster's last statement is anything to go by, it seems to point to the murderer being a stranger who Pat did not know. Webster also reckons the weapon used to stab the girl could have been a run-of-the-mill kitchen knife, but looks more like wounds left from a bayonet or large clasp knife – something akin to the military issue of the folding British Army knife. On the subject of the stab wounds, he thinks Pat may have been unconscious when she was stabbed about the face and neck. This is due to the lack of blood spurting when the child's neck arteries were severed. The unconscious victim's heart rate would have slowed, thus not providing the pressure for the blood to spurt from such ruptured arteries. Webster suggests the sequence of the attack was, firstly the child was suddenly and violently grabbed, then strangled and beaten around the head, and finally pushed into the ground and stabbed, with the knife wounds being contained in a small, but rapid, cluster.

It makes for grim reading. Garner had already seen the horrific injuries inflicted on the child, so he expected the report to be brutal in its detail. Webster has, however, provided Garner with evidence to back up a hunch that he and Chief Inspector Barratt have been mulling over for the past day. They need to speak again with the soldiers on Riddlesworth Camp.

TUESDAY 12ᵀᴴ MAY, 1942

Derby Daily Telegraph – *Child murder search. The police have narrowed down inquiries to seeking three or four people who it is thought might provide valuable information.*

Daily Mirror – *Dead Girl. Tramp sought. Police wish to interview a man of the tramp class.*

Nottingham *Evening Post* – *Evacuee child's death. Reports have been received of experts at Hendon and Nottingham police laboratories, who have examined a weapon which is believed to have been used and articles of Pat's clothing.*

Despite all the newspaper speculation, no murder weapon has been found, although Chief Inspector Barratt's investigation is thorough, leaving no stone unturned. Today he is following up on the statement Constable Gaskin wrote down for him yesterday, namely about a soldier from Riddlesworth Camp, who, while in a Garboldisham pub, made a statement about planning a murder. Even though it may have been the beer talking, it nonetheless has to be treated seriously and followed up. Corporal Wilfred Watkins, admits to being that soldier. Watkins recalls he and some mates were drinking beer and playing cards together in the Swan pub until closing time. He reckons he ended up spending £3 10s on rounds of beer, although some of it was spent on those men who lost their money to him during their card games. He then suggests there was an argument between the soldiers, and a remark was made about the murder of another girl who was killed nearby, but it wasn't about Pat. He cannot remember saying anything about planning the murder of Pat, and in any case if he had then it was simply the beer talking and not something he would have normally said. He also admits to fighting with the other soldiers after he had left the pub. Needless to say, Barratt takes a very dim view of this man, nonetheless the serviceman is not treated as a suspect.

Barratt also catches up with Private Albert Woodbridge, who was on work detail under the supervision of Corporal Molson. Woodbridge was set to work on the ammunition dump with Privates Wyeth and Morgan. Barratt is keen to understand the movements of Wyeth that morning and Woodbridge tells Barratt he was there when Wyeth asked Molson for permission to go to the latrine and that permission was given. He was also present when Wyeth returned.

"Wyeth was perspiring – there were beads of sweat on his forehead – and the boys commented upon this. Apart from perspiring, Wyeth appeared to be his usual self. Wyeth normally has a red face and often sweats freely. He sweats when he works as a rule."

Woodbridge also confirms what the others had told the police, in saying he never saw the girl while he was working that morning. In fact, he had never seen her on any given day.

The police gather more statements that day, but they don't really amount to much. Inspector Dye catches up with Private Sidney Broadhurst, showing the soldier a photograph of a handkerchief that had been found on Riddlesworth Park. The soldier accepts it is his - his wife had stitched the letters, 'S', 'I' and 'D' in one corner. Broadhurst says he lost some of his handkerchiefs while stationed at Riddlesworth, but on the morning in question he was away from the area, and instead was at Southwood Camp on work detail. It seems more than one person saw a man, or men, punting along the Little Ouse River, a river that borders the park, but hadn't thought much about reporting it before now. A teenage student from Riddlesworth Hall, also comes forward to report seeing a man cycling along the dirt track at 8.05am on the morning of the attack.

Before the war, Staff Sergeant Edward Crome, had been an accountancy assistant, but now he is serving in the Royal Engineers and had been stationed at Riddlesworth Camp since August last year. Three days before the attack on Pat, he was reassigned to another camp, twenty-three miles away, at Freckenham, near Mildenhall, Suffolk, so, as such, he is not treated as a suspect. He has seen the appeal for witnesses to come forward with information about Pat or any suspicious sightings near the park, so has volunteered to give a statement informing the police he often saw Pat while he was at Riddlesworth. He was billeted away from the camp and enjoyed lodging with Mr and Mrs Saville, Mr Saville being a gardener at Riddlesworth Hall. Crome often met Pat along the track as he walked to the base. He says she was sometimes with a woman on a cycle, sometimes a small boy was with them. He describes seeing Pat often dressed in a red/brown coat and a similar coloured hat. The woman would always say, "Good morning" to him and the girl would often follow this up with, "Hello". He never saw Pat with anyone else, nor did he ever see her away from the track, specifically never in the bushes nor on the park itself, just on the track, usually with the woman.

Today has seen a flurry of people come forward to offer information. Only they will know why they did not come forward earlier, nonetheless they are at least reporting it now. Perhaps they have been prompted by the recent media publicity? Perhaps, due to no obvious arrests being reported, these people think the investigation has stalled and are eager to offer something that may assist the police. What they are not aware of, or perhaps anyone else for that matter, is the police are closing in on a lead and that the next two days will see a momentous breakthrough.

WEDNESDAY 13TH MAY, 1942

Nottingham Evening Post – *Child Murder Search. Farms and shooting boxes were visited, and a second examination was made of a secluded boathouse on a bank of the Ouse.*

Hartlepool Northern Daily Mail – *Police hopeful that quest is ending. Children at a village school were questioned yesterday, and the living quarters at a military camp were searched and soldiers interrogated.*

Gloucester Citizen – *Child murder search. The police are hopeful that the end of their quest is near.*

Today sees the police scaling down their efforts of interviewing as many people as possible, and instead explore a person of interest. The detectives head out to catch up with a serviceman billeted on the army camp at Southwood, but who was at Riddlesworth Park on the day Pat was attacked. Private Francis Montague had previously reported seeing nothing suspicious to the police, but now they want his version of events, not because they think he is the attacker, but because something someone else said just doesn't add up. They obtain another statement from Montague, which on the surface adds nothing new to the police investigation, however it cannot be further from the truth. While at Riddlesworth, Montague had been tasked with cleaning the army huts where the soldiers slept and kept their possessions. The huts are close to each other, some positioned at right angles, meaning you can stand in one hut and have a clear line of sight to the entrance doors of neighbouring huts. Montague saw no one return to the huts on the morning of the attack. No one. A point he makes very clear in his statement:

"During the time I was cleaning the six section huts, none of the men who occupied those huts returned. I know all the men. They are all in my section. If any had returned whilst I was there, I should have seen them as it is part of my duty, apart from cleaning the huts, to look after them and see that nobody enters them except an occupant who might return for something."

This proves decisive. During the police investigation, one soldier in particular claimed he had returned to his hut for something, but now there is clear evidence disputing this. It looks like someone has lied, but why? It needs to be investigated further. The only other statement taken today is not from a soldier. Nor is it taken from a civilian. Under oath, Detective Sergeant George Willis provides his statement while at Thetford Police Station. Here it is, in full:

"I am Detective Sergeant in the West Suffolk Constabulary, stationed at Bury St. Edmunds. On 12th May, 1942, I received a communication from Chief Inspector Barratt by telephone, and as a result I went to the Sanitary Laundry, Bury St. Edmunds. I there saw the manageress, Mrs Cunliffe, and in her presence made a search of various Military clothing there, and took out a shirt, pair of pants, vest and a pair of socks, which bore the laundry mark Ø42. I took possession of these articles and on the 13th May, 1942, at 4.30pm, I handed them to Detective Inspector Garner at Thetford, together with a laundry ticket, also given to me by Mrs Cunliffe. This bears the name of Pte J. Wyeth, Regt. No. 13089701.

THURSDAY 14TH MAY, 1942

Although the newspapers have been covering Pat's attack since it happened, for some reason their editions are void of any mention of it today. They can be forgiven for thinking there have been no significant breakthroughs, after all, on the surface, the investigation seems to be stalling. However, they are unaware of the developments happening behind the scenes.

Private James Wyeth's laundry has been seized and sent for forensic testing, to look for any microscopic signs of blood or fibres that may indicate he was at the scene of the attack. It seems his version of events simply doesn't add up and has left questions about where he was at the time Pat was attacked. Chief Inspector Barratt is not satisfied that Wyeth has been telling him the whole truth, or any truth for that matter. With Wyeth now being the focus of the investigation, the police – Barratt, along with Detective Inspector Garner and Detective Sergeant Webb; re-visit him at Riddlesworth Camp, although he is now billeted at nearby Southwood Camp and is transported between the two to work. Barratt informs the soldier:

"Your explanation of your movements on the 5th May is not satisfactory and I want you to collect your kit and come with me whilst further enquiries are made."

Wyeth looks at Barratt, and replies simply:

"All right."

Before they leave, Barratt wants to collect all of Wyeth's belongings, so they take the short car journey over to Southwood Camp, where Wyeth leads the police to a tent, inside which a pile of blankets with Wyeth's rusty knife lies on top. Barratt ensures the knife is taken with him. Then, all four men travel by car to Thetford police station where the soldier is placed in a room adjoining the station office. Barratt asks him:

"*You know who I am?*" to which, Wyeth replies he does. Barratt goes further:

"*I have made enquiries into the statement you made on Sunday as to your movements on the morning of 5th May and am not satisfied with your explanation. Is there anything else you can tell me or any person I can see to enable me to satisfy myself that what you have told me is true?*"

Wyeth replies, again without elaborating:

"*I've told you the truth.*"

Offering no corroborative witnesses to support his version of events, Wyeth does not satisfy Barratt's concerns. The detective then informs Wyeth that a new set of clothes has been sent for, and Wyeth will need to stay in the room until the clothing has been delivered and Wyeth can change into them. A short while later, perhaps considering the severity of the situation, Wyeth speaks to Barratt,

"*I remember now, sir, that I took my denim blouse off when I went to the lavatory that morning, and on my way back from the lavatory I dropped it on my bunk in the hut. I saw Montague, the billet orderly, either at break or at dinner that day and he told me he had found it and put it away in my valise for me."*

The reference to blouse is a wartime one, although we might consider it to be a heavy green shirt, worn like a light jacket. Barratt responds by telling Wyeth enquiries will be made to assess the accuracy of this latest story. At 12.15pm, the new clothes from Southwood Camp are delivered for Wyeth. Barratt tells the serviceman to remove all his clothing, including underwear, and put on the new garments. Detective Inspector Garner, who is also in the room, takes Wyeth's clothing, as the serviceman removes them, and proceeds to label them, one by one, in preparation for them to be sent for forensic examination. A telephone call is then made to a police forensic scientist, Dr Henry Smith Holden. Holden is more than a forensic scientist, in fact he has an impressive CV – a Doctor of Science and a Fellow of the Royal Society of Edinburgh; he is also the Director of the Home Office Laboratory, based in Nottingham. The call requests the presence of Holden to come to Thetford to collect the clothing, then take it away for examination for any markers that might point to Wyeth being at the scene of the attack on Pat. The doctor promptly leaves Nottingham and five hours later arrives at Thetford police station.

While all this is happening, Detective Sergeant Albert Webb, Barratt's colleague from New Scotland Yard, remains at Southwood Camp. He is looking for members of Wyeth's work group, to enquire about the suspect's attire on the morning of the attack, so makes a beeline for Corporal Molson, and Privates Montague and Woodbridge. The reply from Woodbridge is that Wyeth was wearing his army issue denim blouse over his battledress tunic, which is what most men did anyway. Woodbridge cannot recall if Wyeth returned from the toilet wearing it, but in all likelihood, he thinks he did. This statement mirrors Molson's recollection, in that Wyeth wore his denim over his battledress. Molson also suggests some soldiers, when getting hot, prefer to work in shirt sleeves, but have to remove their denim and battledress to do so, which Wyeth had not done that morning. He thinks Wyeth remained in denim throughout his work detail. Montague, the soldier in charge of cleaning the huts that morning, is asked if he had seen any uniform left lying around in the huts. He hadn't.

Word gets to Detective Sergeant Webb, that Wyeth has mentioned Private Montague in his latest statement, suggesting Montague found the suspect's denim blouse on the morning Pat was attacked. Montague has something to say about that, which forms his second statement of today:

"I know Private Wyeth very well. When we were at Riddlesworth Camp he used to sleep in the bunk under me.

On the 5th May, 1942, when I was billet orderly, I did not find a denim blouse belonging to Wyeth in the hut or on his bed and put it away for him. I did not tell him that I had found his denim blouse left out and put it away for him.

I am positive I should have remembered this incident had it occurred. I am certain I never found Wyeth's denim blouse and put it away for him."

THE CONFESSION

At 4pm, Chief Inspector Thomas Barratt returns to James Wyeth, who is still sitting alone in the room at Thetford police station. The suspect is told Private Montague has sworn under oath that, despite Wyeth saying his colleague had found his denim blouse, Montague did not say or do such a thing. So, what did Wyeth have to say about that? The soldier says nothing. He has no answer. He takes a short while to ponder a response, then asks Barratt:

"Can I have an hour to think over what I did?"

The police are unsure what Wyeth means when he refers to what he did, nonetheless they leave the serviceman alone to mull it over. At 5.55pm, Wyeth requests to speak with Barratt. Garner and Webb are also in attendance. Barratt approaches Wyeth and says:

"I understand you want to see me."

Barratt has prepared himself for what comes next, bringing a piece of paper with him. On the paper is printed the text forming the official police caution. Without allowing Wyeth time to say anything, Barratt reads the caution to the serviceman, telling him he should know that anything he goes on to say will be taken down in writing and given in evidence. Wyeth replies:

"*Yes sir, I want to tell you I went with the girl, and all I can remember what I done to her.*"

Immediately, Barratt stops Wyeth talking anymore and gets him to sign the paper with the formal caution printed on it. After signing it, Wyeth goes on to explain what happened with him and Pat. Barratt knows the procedure from here on in, so he writes down Wyeth's words in his notepad. It will form Wyeth's confession. Wyeth will of course need to sign the confession, stating he is happy it truthfully represents what he has just said. Barratt offers to read it back to Wyeth, or at least allow Wyeth the opportunity to read it through himself. Wyeth elects the latter. When Barratt is certain Wyeth has finished reading it through, the detective asks if it truthfully represents what the serviceman had just confessed.

"*Yes,*" Wyeth replies.

"*Well, write down that you have read the statement and it is all true.*"

Wyeth hesitates, "*Is there anything else?*"

Barratt answers, "*Is there anything else you wish to say?*"

"*Only that I am glad to get it off my mind.*"

"*Well, write that if you want to, and sign it.*"

In the presence of Chief Inspector Thomas Barratt,

also witnessed by Detective Inspector William Garner and Detective Sergeant Albert Webb, Wyeth signs the following statements:

"*I have been cautioned by Chief Inspector Barratt that I am not obliged to say anything unless I wish to and that what I say will be taken down in writing and may be given in evidence.*

(SIGNED) J. Wyeth."

"*I have thought about what I done, and I want to tell you what happened.*

When I was working on the ammunition shed with Corporal Molson's working party on Tuesday, 5th May, 1942, just after we started work in the morning about 8, I saw a little girl go past the house on the footpath near where we were working. She was dressed in a pink coat. I had a feeling come over me to follow her.

I had a bad head that morning, and I was feeling rough. I wanted to follow the girl, so I asked Corporal Molson if I could go to the lavatory. He told me I could, so I went down the path towards the lavatories, and when I got past the N.A.A.F.I. canteen and nearly to my hut, I turned off into the woods towards the park, past where the girl had gone. When I got out of the wood into the park, I saw the little girl on the path about halfway across the park. I cut across the field towards the girl and followed her until she reached a clump of trees. I then got hold of the girl's clothes at the back of her neck and dragged her under the trees out of sight. I don't remember any more until I saw her lying on her back in front of me with blood all over her face.

I was frightened when I saw this. I jumped up and covered her up with a piece of sacking or something which was on the ground nearby. I then ran back to the Camp across the park over the ditch. I went through the wooden fence into the wood and came out on to the track near the N.A.A.F.I. As I turned to walk towards where we were working, I saw Corporal Molson. He said to me, "What about some work being done?" and I told him I had been to the lavatory. I started work and then it dawned on me that I had done something terribly wrong. I looked at my hands and clothes but couldn't see any blood on them.

I felt very depressed after that, and then had a bad toothache; this lasted for three days. I have felt very worried and depressed ever since. I can't concentrate like I could.

I have read this statement and it is all true, and glad to get it off my mind.

(SIGNED) James Wyeth"

Wyeth's only reaction is to sit in silence, head hung low. Barratt asks him if there is anything else to say, but

Wyeth remains silent. After a few minutes of this, he turns to Barratt once more and makes an extraordinary offer to the detective:

"*I can't remember anything else, sir, but I can take you and show you where I went.*"

Sensing more revelations, Barratt advises Wyeth that he is still under caution, and repeats that Wyeth should understand that anything he goes on to say or do will continue to be taken down and used as evidence. Wyeth, with a simple, "Yes", acknowledges this. Barratt, striking while the iron is hot, and also hoping to visit the scene of the attack before it gets dark, takes Wyeth, along with Garner and Webb, to Riddlesworth Park.

RE-VISITING THE SCENE OF THE ATTACK

The police car carrying the four men pulls up near Mr Tortice's cottage. Once parked, they exit the car and walk to the ammunition dump where Wyeth was working on the morning Pat was attacked. Barratt is keen to understand Wyeth's movements from this point, so he asks the serviceman to take the lead. Wyeth is more than happy to co-operate and the group follow him up a northerly track into Riddlesworth army camp. As they walk through the camp, it is obvious the other servicemen know what is happening. The four men move to behind the N.A.A.F.I.

canteen hut and take a right turn, to follow a different track through the forest, one that takes them away from the camp and onto Riddlesworth Park. At the edge of the forest, Wyeth slips through the wooden fence, followed by the others. From this point he could not see how far Pat had walked, what with the foliage obscuring the track somewhat, so he made a beeline straight toward the track. He goes on to show them how he traversed a meadow and a ditch to arrive at the track, with Pat a short distance ahead. The group continues along the track toward the site of the attack, and within five yards of where the girl's hat was found, Wyeth stops the group.

"*This is where I caught her,*" he tells them.

He then retraces his steps from that fateful day, stooping under the low branches of a tree to stop at where he left Pat's limp body. He seems confused, in his mind something has changed, he says:

"*I think this is the place, but there was some bushes here.*"

Wyeth is not aware the police have subsequently removed those bushes to assist them in their forensic search for the weapon. It indicates to Barratt the man has not visited the scene of the crime since the attack. At this point, there is no doubt in Barratt's mind that Wyeth, who has been very compliant so far, is the person who brutally attacked little Pat.

Wyeth, after showing the men how he approached, or rather stalked, the child, now takes the group back to the camp, on the route he took after attacking Pat. This time he does not follow the track and instead shows them a more direct one, over meadows and a couple of ditches, thus suggesting he ran back to gain as much distance from the attack scene in the shortest amount of time. Once back inside the forest, his route, past the N.A.A.F.I. and on the track toward the ammunition dump, is the same route from where the men started. The group finally return to the police car, with Barratt having made notes throughout. The visit has served its purpose, so they make their way to Thetford Police Station. Once back, Garner tells Wyeth he is to be detained pending further enquiries.

FRIDAY, 15TH MAY, 1942

Daily News – *Dead Evacuee: Man Detained. A man was taken into custody last night.*

Liverpool Echo – *Soldier questioned by police. A soldier who was detained for questioning at Thetford, Norfolk, last night was still at the police station to-day.*

Daily Mirror – *Tramp sees police. A tramp the police were anxious to question for information in connection with the murder of Pat Ann Cupit has been found and questioned, but was not detained.*

James Wyeth, who has spent the night at Thetford police station, is met by Chief Inspector Barratt and Detective Inspector Garner at 12.40pm. It is Garner, of the Norfolk Country Constabulary, who formerly charges the prisoner:

"On the 6th May, 1942, I saw the dead body of Pat Ann Cupit at Bury St. Edmunds Hospital. As a result of enquiries which have been made, you will be charged, for that you, on Tuesday, the 5th May, 1942, at Riddlesworth Park, did murder Pat Ann Cupit."

Garner then proceeds to caution Wyeth, but at no point does the soldier respond. Events rapidly progress. Ninety minutes later, at 2pm, Wyeth is stood before Henry Watling Esq., Thetford's Mayor, but in this instance, Watling is serving as Chairman of the Occasional Court, inside Thetford police station. Another magistrate, Sir William Gentle, is also sitting, while Captain Stephen Van Neck, Chief Constable of Norfolk County Constabulary has rushed over from Norwich to attend too. Garner briefly outlines the case and Watling, who has read through Wyeth's confession, has no option but to remand the prisoner in custody. The prisoner is to be held at Norwich prison, with a view to appearing at the Petty Sessions in East Harling, Norfolk, at 10.30am, on Monday, 1st June, 1942. Norwich prison is informed, that upon receiving Wyeth, the prisoner needs to be kept under psychiatric observation.

Half-an-hour after the court hearing, the forensic scientist, Dr Henry Smith Holden who arrived yesterday to receive the prisoner's clothing, leaves Thetford destined back to Nottingham to carry out his tests. He informs the police his report will be available in a couple of working days.

Detective Inspector Barratt can now feel some level of satisfaction that he has apprehended Pat's attacker, yet he knows his work is far from done. There is the court hearing to prepare for. There are more statements to be gathered from local residents and soldiers. Wyeth's background needs investigation. Then, there will be requests from both the prosecution and defence lawyers. The list of work to be done is almost endless. News of Pat's murder has once again caught the attention of the nation, so Barratt knows he will have to face the inevitable onslaught of reporters clamouring for details. The police release information of the man charged with murdering Pat, leading to some of the late editions naming James Wyeth.

STOP PRESS!

Dundee Evening Telegraph – *James Wyeth (21), soldier, was at Thetford, Norfolk, this afternoon remanded until June 1 charged with the murder of Pat Ann Cupit, 6½-year old London evacuee found stabbed on May 5. Detective-*

Inspector Garner stated that Wyeth told him at Thetford police station yesterday – "can you get Chief Detective Barratt. I want to tell him that I did it".

PART TWO – PREPARING FOR TRIAL

James Wyeth, after being charged with murdering Pat, was immediately sent to Norwich prison to be detained on remand. He was one of five men who arrived yesterday. The other four have already had their fates decided, after passing through local magistrates' hearings. Compared to Wyeth's charge of murder, their crimes are far less serious, ranging from 42 days detention for "breach of naval discipline", to someone going AWOL from a ship, also another who has breached his bail after being found guilty of theft.

Today, the Norwich prison governor writes in his daily journal. He mentions the five men received yesterday, also two others who were released. He logs the current number of inmates at 119, the majority being local men typically facing a few weeks or months there for 'petty' crime, and a few servicemen held for minor military transgressions. Already, since his arrival, Wyeth has become notorious within the prison, as reflected by the Governor making a special comment in his journal. He rarely singles out a prisoner, but does so on this occasion:

"No. 1293, J Wyeth was received here yesterday on remand on a murder charge."

Wyeth's time at Norwich will see him having no wish to interact with anyone. For the most part he will remain silent and keep himself to himself. He may be withdrawn, feeling safer within his own world, but this will be tested by the occasional air raid siren, a reminder that even Norwich prison, and Wyeth's solitude, is not immune from the war's reach. On 27th June the prison will receive a direct hit from a 100lb bomb dropped from an enemy aircraft. Although buildings are damaged, but no one is injured, the Governor responds by sending 15 of the longer-serving inmates off to Lincoln prison, just to ease pressure on accommodation in Norwich. Wyeth, not having been convicted, will remain at Norwich to endure more air raid sirens.

MONDAY, 18TH MAY, 1942

Despite the media clamouring for details, the police issued the briefest of statements confirming James Wyeth as having been arrested at Thetford for Pat's murder. They then merely quoted his age and his request to speak to Chief Inspector Thomas Barratt. It seems they have used the media to publicise their appeal for witnesses and garner sympathy for the case, but for the time being, this support is no longer needed. In fact, compared to the level of detail reported immediately following the attack, news of the arrest is largely subdued.

Some daily regional newspapers print a syndicated report based on the police briefing, and even the *Daily Mirror*, who previously gained exclusive access to Pat's parents, confine themselves to that brief report. There is no doubt the newspapers' interest will peak again, at various points of this story, but for now they are more concerned with developments in the war, especially the Russians taking on the Germans, and the Japanese threat in the Far East.

Back at Thetford police station, Chief Inspector Barratt, who spent the weekend back home in London, and Detective Inspector William Garner meet up with Edwin Graham, a surveyor employed by Norfolk County Council. Mr Graham has been tasked with providing a scale map of key locations in the murder case, along with the route Pat took and where her body was found. The three men travel together, heading to Riddlesworth Park.

Mr Graham spends the day mapping out the park. The map he goes on to create is so precise - an exact scale drawing of 208.33 feet to the inch; it can guide any courtroom judge and jury along the route that Pat and her assailant took. It also shows the relationships between key locations in the attack, such as Tortice's Lodge, the ammunition dump, Wyeth's hut on the camp, the latrines Wyeth initially alleged he visited and the track Pat used when she walked to school. Graham measures the total distance of Pat's walk from the Pasks' home to school as being a distance of 1.2 miles. At 0.8 miles she was discovered laying in Ladies Grove, indicated on the map with a red cross.

It is now two days since Wyeth was charged. Over the weekend, the police discovered he had been to borstal, specifically Feltham, a young offender institution, before enlisting into the army. They also uncover the fact his release from borstal was conditional, on licence, meaning any bad behaviour from him would see him detained again. His signed confession, an admission to attacking a young girl, provides evidence that he has broken the rules of his licence. Normally those on remand are viewed as innocent until proven guilty in a court of law, but in Wyeth's case it seems he is guilty of breaking his parole, before he even gets to stand trial for murder. Norwich prison is informed of this, in addition to receiving an instruction to keep Wyeth under psychiatric observation. Barratt now begins the arduous task of making enquiries as to the circumstance of why Wyeth was in borstal and if he has had further encounters with the police.

TUESDAY, 19TH MAY, 1942

Before the war, the population in and around Riddlesworth numbered less than 300 people, scattered in small hamlets around the park. Since the police investigation began, more than 200 people have given statements, some willingly stepping forward, while others were sought and some have been visited more than once. There can be few adults, locals or soldiers, who have not been spoken to by the police. Yet, even though the police seemingly have in their custody the man responsible for the attack, there are further statements to be written down. Chief Inspector Barratt is keen to understand Wyeth's behaviour in the days following the attack on Pat and he knows such knowledge will only be gained by speaking to those who served with the serviceman. Barratt invites those soldiers to visit him today at Thetford Police Station.

Corporal Edward Molson tells Barratt that, a couple of days after the attack, Wyeth complained of having toothache and asked to be excused from work. At the time, the corporal suggested to Wyeth he take some aspirin to ease the pain, even offering to buy them himself when Wyeth said he had no money. In fact, this is what Molson ended up doing. He still believes Wyeth's toothache was genuine. The corporal even relieved Wyeth from the task of peeling potatoes so the man could go and lay down. Barratt asks Molson if he saw any injuries on Wyeth, or if the man's behaviour changed after the attack on Pat. Molson replies:

"He has never complained to me of any injury he has

received, and I have no knowledge that at any time he has received any injury.

Wyeth is normally of a quiet type, and has been particularly so since the seventh of May. I have put this down to him having toothache."

Another soldier, who came to Thetford to comment on Wyeth's attitude, was Private Albert Woodbridge. Woodbridge had known Wyeth for eight months and confirmed him as being a loner, someone who was moody and not the talkative type. It was not uncommon for Wyeth to not speak to anyone for two or three days straight. Yes, Woodbridge was also aware that Wyeth had complained of toothache, but this was a day or two after the attack, not on the day itself. Barratt asks Woodbridge if Wyeth ever carried a weapon of any sort during his work, or even something that could be used as a weapon. Woodbridge did recall seeing Wyeth with a pair of pliers, but these were given for the task of taking down the ammunition dump. Other than that, he hadn't seen anything he would recognise as being a weapon.

Someone else who was questioned whether Wyeth was seen carrying a weapon was Private Tom Windle. Windle was the closest to a friend that Wyeth had in the army, although in truth Wyeth never let anyone get close to him. The pair first met in early February this year, when Windle was sent to Cromer, Norfolk, just a week after enlisting with the Pioneer Corps. It was in Cromer that they shared a billet and had continued to do so since. Windle claims he and Wyeth would often leave camp to go out in the evening. While at Riddlesworth, they would usually spend their evenings together in the N.A.A.F.I., although on one occasion they did visit nearby Thetford. He recalls the event in his statement:

"*I think it was Saturday, the 25ᵗʰ April, 1942, we arrived in Thetford at about 4pm and after having a look round the town and having a drink together, Wyeth suddenly said, 'I'm going back to camp'. I asked him why and he replied, 'There's nothing here. Are you coming with me?' I said 'No. I'm staying here'. When I arrived back at camp that night Wyeth was not there. This was about 11.30pm. He came in about a quarter of an hour later and said he had been to a dance hall in Thetford.*"

After that night, the two of them preferred to stay on camp and spend evenings in the N.A.A.F.I., but on the weekend before the attack, Windle and a few others asked Wyeth if he wanted to go back into Thetford with them. He turned them down. He did however, on the evening after the attack, go to the N.A.A.F.I., although he declined an invitation to continue on to a dance in the nearby village of Hopton, just a 10-minute drive away. This dance was significant for the soldiers because some of them, including Windle and Wyeth, were being relocated to Southwood Camp, near Thetford, in the morning, so they saw it as a farewell to Riddlesworth. Windle recalled:

"*I asked him if he would come with me to Hopton to a dance but he refused. I went off at about 7.15pm, leaving him in the hut. I got back at about 11pm and Wyeth was then in his bed. Most of the chaps in the hut had packed their valises ready for moving the next day, and I found that my valise had been packed for me. I unpacked my valise the following morning to get some cigarettes out and found nothing unusual with my kit. The only thing I noticed was that five cigarettes were missing, but I did not say anything to him about this.*

Since moving to Southwood Camp, Wyeth has refused to come out with me in the evenings as he used to do and would not visit the N.A.A.F.I. at Snare Hill, Southwood, with me when I went."

It seems the only exception to Wyeth not going out was on Friday 8th May, when he was so desperate for cigarettes that he briefly popped over to the N.A.A.F.I. to get some. Barratt enquires if Windle ever saw Wyeth carrying a knife around camp. The soldier responds:.

"*One day, since we have been at Southwood Camp, Wyeth said he had lost his dinner knife and I lent him mine. Later that same day he showed me his knife and said he had found it in his kit. I have never known Wyeth to carry his dinner knife when he was going to Southwood Camp from Riddlesworth. None of us carried it as a rule because we always had sandwiches. Wyeth has, on a few occasions, borrowed my jack knife to cut his sandwiches.*

Although I was friendly with Wyeth, I found him a strange sort of chap and very moody, particularly since Saturday, the 2nd May, 1942.

He never seemed to have any interest in girls when he was out with me."

Away from gathering statements, today also sees the release of Dr Henry Smith Holden's forensic report on both Pat's and Wyeth's clothing. It is no surprise he finds blood on Pat's, but his report on Wyeth's denim trousers and denim blouse highlights the following, thus providing more evidence of Wyeth's involvement in the attack.

"A number of small splashes of human blood is present on the left and right legs of the denim trousers in the positions marked. A similar blood splash is present on the edge of the side pocket on the left side, and slight blood smears are present on the lining of the long pocket on the front of the left leg.

I removed a number of fibres from the right sleeve of the denim blouse near the cuff edge. These are woollen fibres of three kinds, two colourless and one dyed red. They show detailed agreement with fibres taken by me for comparison from the child's pink coat. I also removed a single red fibre from the edge of the left cuff of the woollen khaki pullover, which agrees exactly with red fibres taken from the pink coat."

LETTERS TO MRS CUPIT

THURSDAY, 21ˢᵀ MAY, 1942

Today, Chief Inspector Barratt's attention is distracted by something raised by his counterparts at Norbury police station, London. Pat's parents live within the catchment of Norbury and her mother, Anne Cupit, has today raised a formal complaint there. The reason for the complaint started on the day Wyeth confessed to attacking her daughter.

That day, Anne received a small envelope, sent in the post. This was not unusual as there had been much outpouring of sympathy to the parents of the murdered child. In the top left corner of this particular envelope the word 'urgent' had been hand written, and whoever sent it had omitted Anne's house number, but no doubt the local postmen, due to the publicity Pat's murder had generated, knew exactly where the Cupits lived. Also, because the tragedy had appeared so prominently in newspapers across Britain, even people unknown to Anne were sending letters of sympathy. This looked like such a letter. She opened it. Inside were four small sheets of lined paper, written on both sides in blue ink, not a biro but a proper ink pen. The sentiment started off reasonably well, neat handwriting, with a sympathetic tone, but halfway through it began a descent into a scruffy scrawl, making it difficult to read. The words, sometimes with bad spelling, were part joined-up handwriting and part capital letters, full stops littered the sentences and were not always where they needed to be. The text also became menacing, making accusations about who had killed Pat and what needed to happen to that person. As Anne read through, it became clear the writer was emotionally charged.

"*May.13.5.1942*

Dear Mr & Mrs Cupit.

This is Wednesday, I've just been reading the newspapers and I've just come across the brutal murder of your daughter, Pat. To me you seem to be a young married couple. I know what it is for you to be separated from your husband & Baby. I now see that your child was to (sic) young to leave you, no matter how hard the war affected you. Some kiddies are put on people and they don't want them. Some don't know what bombing of a town's like anyway your husband wants revenge. Is he back at his unit yet if not or if so inform him. I have a warning to give to you. Take courage and confidence but you will sure come through alright. Death has no sting. Send your husband to that Mr A Pask. In the paper it said he was the first to find Pat. Well look here lass the one that hides can always find. I'm a reader of the destiny of life from the face & hand. I only wished I could kill people more but you can't with the war on because it affects peoples life line.

*Now your husband can go to him and say, here it is, What did Pat say when she was supposed to have left you that MORNING WHEN SHE STARTED FOR SCHOOL. Mr. Pask. WHERE WAS you when Pat left. Take action according to what he says. If he says he was at a certain place go AND SEE IF HE WAS. FEAR I've got the culprit. **MR PASK – the MURDERER.***

You can THEN TAKE JUDGEMENT FROM the FACE. IT SEEMS queer no one hearing HER SHOUT. I READ SHE was very shy. Well this person definitely had a lot to say to Pat, MR. PASK FOUND HER IN THE AFTERNOON alive WHEN anyone does a job like that it plays ON THE MIND. Look here MR PASK is aFRAID. The police on other MURDERS have looked for days and NEVER found THEM. So in the eyes of GOD. MR PASK. comes forward now it's for you to start on him.

I do hope I've helped you, mine is a great revenge, you have me to back you up all the more. I remain to you as Miss Gwen Salter. Au revoir

P.S. KEEP on this MR PASK HE'LL give WAY. TIME ONLY TELLS THIS WILL SURPRISE YOU."

Understandably, the letter shook Anne to her core. She broke down. What grounds could a stranger, who knew nothing of the family, or indeed of Mr Pask, make such an accusation? It seemed the writer, claiming her psychic abilities as a clairvoyant, or as she termed it, a *"reader of the destiny of life"*, allowed her to see things that others could not. At the time, Anne did not react, perhaps not knowing the best response to make, but then perhaps her attention was more focused on the fact a man had that day confessed to attacking her daughter. That man was not Mr Pask. Not for a second had Anne believed Mr Pask was involved, after all, they had all shared the emotional turmoil after her daughter's death. He had effectively lost his foster daughter, a child given to him to care for. The letter was simply put away and ignored.

That was until another letter from Gwen, was delivered to Anne a couple of days ago, this time dated 18th May, 1942. Again, the writer demonstrated a lack of knowledge about the case and seemed to have merely picked up snippets from reading the newspapers.

"Dear Mrs Cupit.

I have accused Mr Pask Murderer of your Pat. This I can never turn back on. I see now they have in custody until June 1st a soldier named James Wyeth 21 years old. I can only judge by sight or by way of papers.

The Sunday Pictorial said Pat had a mile and a half to walk to school through a park and Mr Pask found her in the afternoon covered over by a bag. How did Mr Pask know she had not been to school and other little lasses that have been murdered it's taken the police a long time to find them. Perhaps this soldier has been at camp with the rest of the lads and the murder of your lass has played on his mind. Still time only will tell.

This is to me a strange affair and we have to wait and see what happens. I read in the paper a few years back of a man lodging with a married woman and the kiddies had taken to him as their uncle and one as she was coming home from school this man met her and took her on a bus. Supposed to have taken her to her aunties but he lured her to his old cottage and while in bed he strangled her and tied her body in a sack and by weights he sank her in a river. The police looked high and low but after a good many months the sack gave way and the body was found floating on the river. I just cant remember this man or little girl's name but I know the man paid for it on the gallows. I can work on this soldier only by the statement he gives the police when he's charged. Anyway its very doubtful. I am certain Mr Pask is in some way connected with it. Him finding her. So I am hoping you may send me a line back. I remain to you as Gwen Salter."

Anne notices in both letters that Gwen gives her address - Vicarage Bank, Chebsey, in Staffordshire; perhaps hoping for a reply. Anne does indeed react, but not in the way Gwen is hoping. Today, instead of writing back to Gwen, a distressed Anne takes both letters to her local police station. In turn, Norbury police station contact the man leading the investigation into Pat's murder, Chief Inspector Barratt. In due course, Barratt will receive these letters and likewise be appalled at what he reads. On 26th May, 1942, he will send a strongly worded telegram to the Superintendent of Staffordshire County Constabulary, in Stone, just a few miles from where Gwen lives. Not long after, the police will arrive at Gwen's home to discover a 22-year-old single woman, living with her parents on a dairy farm. The police will then inform her that her letters have caused Pat's parents much unneeded suffering and she will have to immediately cease any contact with them. The shock of the police turning up at her parents' farm does the trick. From then on, Anne will no longer receive letters from Gwen.

Pat's parents have had a lot to deal with. Usually, the mourning of a child puts such immense strain on anyone that their mental health suffers badly, but Anne's daughter was taken without notice, so suddenly and so violently, that it makes it all the harder to bear. Anne has also had to endure the police manhunt and the inquisitive newspaper questions. With such a spotlight on her daughter's demise, it has no doubt led her feeling everyone's gaze upon her when she leaves the confines of her home, and conversations being hushed when she enters a room. Perhaps she feels she is not being left to mourn naturally? Now, when it seems the police finally have a suspect, someone has tried to get into her head to cast doubt over who is innocent or guilty. In later years, a family member will report that Anne, in the hours of darkness and while still wearing her night clothes, was often found visiting the grave of her daughter and sobbing uncontrollably.

BARRATT'S REPORT

TUESDAY, 26TH MAY, 1942

Since Chief Inspector Thomas Barratt first arrived at Thetford railway station three weeks ago, he has been meticulously compiling a report which is to be sent to the Director of Public Prosecutions. It is also addressed for the attention of Barratt's superiors at New Scotland Yard, and the Chief Constable of Norfolk County Constabulary, Captain Stephen Van Neck. This formal document will also be handed to any future courtroom judge, defence and prosecution team. As such, it is also classed as formal evidence. Today sees Barratt finish that report and send it off.

In the 26-page report, Barratt describes the backgrounds of Pat, her family and the Pasks. He goes on to describe events following the discovery of the girl's body, including statements made by those who discovered her. There are precise forensic notes, from the scene and a subsequent post-mortem report, carried out by Dr Webster, which makes for grim reading. Barratt details Dr Webster's findings in full:

(1) An incised wound in front of the left ear, vertical in position, the upper extremity of the wound involving the external ear itself. This wound measured 1¼ inches in length and involved not merely the superficial tissues but the deep underlying tissues which had been penetrated.

(2) An incised wound of the outer margin of the left external ear which incompletely severed this margin, the detached portion of the ear still attached at the upper end of the wound. This wound measured 1¼ inches and had severed the skin and part of the cartilage of the external ear.

(3) Immediately behind the external ear on the mastoid portion of the skull was an incised wound, almost vertical in position, measuring 1 inch. This wound had severed not merely the skin but all the underlying tissues down to the bone, the bone being bare.

(4) Immediately below and parallel to the left lower jaw was an incised wound 1½ inches in length. This wound had passed up in front of the jaw bone and communicated with the mouth in front of the teeth, the lining membrane of the lip having been severed. The bone was bare and the tissues along the track of this wound had been cut beyond the extremities of the wound, indicating that the stabbing instrument had not been cleanly plunged in and cleanly pulled out, but had moved considerably whilst still sticking in the body.

(5) An incised wound, much more superficial than any of the previous injuries, upon the left cheek, ⁷/₈ inch in length. This wound had not penetrated to any great depth. At its upper extremity only superficial skin was severed, and the rest of the wound had passed just through the true skin, exposing the underlying fat.

(6) On the point of the chin slightly to the right of the midline there was a T-shaped incised wound, the long line of the T measuring ¾ inch. This did not communicate with the mouth, but led down to bare bone.

In addition to the above incised wounds, there were the following marks of violence: –

Bruising of both eyes. The left upper eyelid had a large amount of blood in it which extended through the whole thickness of the lid, but the bruising of the right eye was much more superficial.

The left side of the face had superficial abrasions upon it such as could have been caused by the face having been knocked against or pressed hard against vegetation lying upon the ground.

On the front of the neck were deep abrasions, semi-lunar in shape, such as could have been caused by and were entirely consistent with pressure from the nails of the hand. From the shape and position of these nail-marks, he (Dr Webster) is of the opinion that two hands had been used and that the child's neck had been grasped from her right side.

On the front of the neck, lower down than the nail marks and extending slightly to both sides of the neck, but completely absent at the back, was a patterned ligature mark outlined as a bruise. This ligature mark Dr Webster compared with the design of the neck of the child's vest, and is of the opinion that this was caused by the vest having been pulled tight against the front of the child's neck, the assailant grasping and pulling the neck-band from behind her.

There were superficial bruising of the front of the left shoulder and upper part of the chest on both sides of the midline.

Both legs were bruised.

On the legs posteriorly, outlined by the post-mortem staining were several round marks, quite superficial, upon the skin, which could have been caused by pressure with the fingers prior to death.

Chief Inspector Barratt also writes in great detail about how the case was investigated, how many people were interviewed and that Wyeth's statements do not align with those of other soldiers. He quotes Wyeth's statements in full and then goes into great detail as to why he believes Wyeth is guilty of attacking Pat.

"(1) Wyeth was working in a position from which he had a good view of the pathway along which the deceased girl always walked to school. Enquiries have failed to disclose that any persons other than Wyeth and his party were in this part of the Camp at the material time.

(2) Wyeth's request to go to the lavatory at the approximate time it is estimated the child would be passing along the path.

(3) Wyeth's return about 40 minutes later, hot and sweating for no obvious reason, and in such a condition as to cause comment by his workmates.

(4) The length of time Wyeth was away from his work was sufficient to enable him to commit this offence at the spot where the girl was discovered and return to the dump. In this connection I would refer to his statement that he walked there and ran back. Detective Sergeant Webb has carried out this journey over the route shown by Wyeth by walking to the spot and running back. He checked his time by a stop watch and found the outward journey took 10 minutes, 10 seconds, and the return journey 7 minutes, 10 seconds. This was checked by me remaining at the dump and timing his departure and return. I would also draw attention to the fact that Wyeth could have left and returned to the camp by a shorter route had he so desired. It will, therefore, be seen that Wyeth would have from fifteen and twenty minutes to commit the offence.

(5) In his statement on the 10th May, 1942, Wyeth stated he had sat on a lavatory for 30 minutes and was sweating on his return due to the walk from the lavatory, and the weather. The weather at that time of the morning – which is actually only about 7 a.m. – could not reasonably be expected to be sufficiently hot as to make him perspire so freely from a short walk after sitting down for half an hour.

(6) Wyeth's statement that he had seen and spoken to

Morgan when leaving his hut to go to the lavatory, which fact is denied by Morgan.

(7) When first interviewed on the 14th May he gave fresh information that he had returned his denim blouse to his hut and that he had been told by Private Montague that the latter had put it away for him. Montague denied any knowledge of this incident.

(8) The scientific evidence relating to the bloodstains on Wyeth's denim trousers.

(9) The scientific evidence of the finding on Wyeth's denim blouse of four fibres corresponding exactly with fibres taken from the girl's coat.

(10) Wyeth's admission. This discloses certain points which, it may be considered, only the person who committed the offence could have had direct knowledge of. These points are as follows: –

(a) That the girl was wearing a pink coat.

(b) That he caught her by the clothes at the back of her neck and dragged her under the trees; this action is consistent with the expressed opinion of Dr Webster as to the manner in which the pressure marks were made on the lower part of the neck of the child by the top of her vest.

(c) That he saw the child's face covered with blood. The head and face were the only parts of the child's body to which *injury had been caused, and when found her face was covered in blood.*

(d) That he covered the body with "sacking or something" which he found on the ground nearby.

(e) When pointing out to the Police the route he took to where he committed the offence, he followed the path along which the girl would normally walk, stopped near the spot where the hat was found and then walked straight to the spot where the body was found.

Within his report, Barratt remains objective, adding no emotion to his sentences, and purely concerning himself with the facts as he understands them to be. However, it is simply the tip of the iceberg. Those reading it will not see the extent of correspondence and telephone calls, the to-ing and fro-ing, with the borstal system, social workers, medical staff, regional police forces, and even Wyeth's family, that Barratt and his team have laboured with since the confession. Barratt could not finish his report until all these people and organisations had been chased up for their responses. Barratt's report also includes Wyeth's previous police record.

JAMES WYETH'S POLICE RECORD

James Wyeth was born on 18th May, 1920, in a small village in South Wales, although Wyeth was not his birth name. His natural mother did not lead a settled life, she instead chose a travelling lifestyle, which often led to her children being neglected for periods of time, perhaps even abused. When she was convicted of child neglect, at around her son's second birthday, he was taken into care and put up for adoption by the National Society for Prevention of Cruelty to Children (NSPCC). It was Charles and Evelyn Wyeth who responded to a newspaper advert and took the boy into their home. Truth be told, this decision was led more by Evelyn and she has always stood by her son, through thick and thin. Wyeth attended school at Pontypridd, South Wales until he reached the age of 14, at which time he left and went into employment.

On 13th August 1935, Wyeth, who was then aged 15 and employed as a houseboy in a local hotel, appeared before the Juvenile Court of Llandrindod Wells after being accused of assaulting a little girl. It seemed he, while pushing his cycle along a road, followed the girl into a field, where he then proceeded to push her over for seemingly no reason other than his own enjoyment. Then, as she lay on the ground, he knelt on top of her, and in order to prevent her screams being heard, he stuffed his handkerchief into, and placed his hand over, her mouth. The poor child was traumatised beyond belief, with Wyeth's actions also leading to her sustaining a cut lip and bruising to the back of her head. He later claimed, in a statement to police:

"*Something seemed to come over me to hit the girl*".

He was fined £5 and bound over for 12 months, for the sum of £10. If he did something like this again within the next year, he would risk a custodial sentence.

In the months following Wyeth's court case, his family moved from Wales to an address in Hereford, but it is not known if this was as a consequence to Wyeth's appearance in court. Nonetheless, his parents would have hoped this move at least offered a fresh start. It needed to, because the family were already trying to make ends meet and their purse strings had been stretched further by paying Wyeth's bond money up front, a sum that equated to over two weeks' wages. With the new start, came a new job for Wyeth, courtesy of his mother who found him employment as an errand boy at Henry Davies' greengrocer shop, in Hereford's High Street. At 5.30pm, on 23rd October, 1935, as Wyeth was out delivering groceries for Mr Davies, he attacked another little girl.

Wyeth had been sent out to deliver groceries to a customer and upon having difficulty finding the address, asked a small girl for directions. She then suggested she would show him where the house was. They had only walked a short distance to a lamp post, when the girl instructed Wyeth on how to get to the house from where they were. It seemed he had made her anxious and she no longer wanted to be near him. She told him:

"*I want to go home now*"

But as she turned and started to walk away, Wyeth, for no apparent reason, hit her in the face. The little girl screamed and managed to run away. He did not give chase, instead he continued looking for the delivery address as though nothing had happened. After delivering the groceries he returned home, not saying a word to anyone about what had happened. The girl was not so silent. In her distressed state, she told her parents, who in turn informed the police. Three days later, policemen visited Wyeth's family home, where he was cautioned about the incident. He gave a statement, signed in the presence of his adoptive father, and a few weeks later, on 13th November 1935, Wyeth appeared at the Hereford County Juvenile Court, accused of assaulting the girl. She was just 7-years-old.

The magistrates found Wyeth guilty, so this should

have triggered his detainment on account of him breaking his bond. However, he was simply bound over again, for another year, this time for only £5, though the magistrates provided an additional condition to his parole. The teenager was subject to the conditions of a Supervision Order, meaning he and his family had to work closely with the local authority to understand his issues, namely why he was bullying little girls. In doing this, the magistrates sought to improve Wyeth's outlook, acknowledging he had mental health problems, rather than punishing him. For his part, Wyeth would have been subjected to certain restrictions, such as regularly checking in with his parole officer. In mitigation, Wyeth apologised to the court:

"I am sorry for knocking this little girl about and will not do it again."

The trouble was, Wyeth did do it again. To make matters worse, it was less than two weeks after he made that promise.

The day was Wednesday 27th November, 1935, while Wyeth was walking to work, where he was still employed at Mr Davies' greengrocer shop. He took a short cut along a path between Tower Road and Broomy Hill in Hereford, where he saw a little girl walking ahead. He caught up with her and said:

"Let's play horses."

In his arms he was carrying a halter, the leather straps that go over a horse's head to enable the animal to be ridden, and he proceeded to place it over the girl's head, as she screamed:

"No, take it off."

He forced her to the ground, face down, and got on top of her, as if to ride her like a horse. Wyeth, then realising the girl's brother was a little way in front, stood up, took the halter off the girl and resumed his walk to work. Perhaps the brother and sister did not report this to their parents, or were unable to identify Wyeth as being the assailant, but for whatever reason the police did not catch up straight away with Wyeth about this. They did, however, catch up with him for his next 'episode', which was later associated with this one.

A couple of weeks later, this time while he was walking home from work, at 4.30pm, on 12th December, 1935, he saw that same little girl who he had tried to ride like a horse. She was stood alone on the pavement. He approached and said:

"Hullo."

The girl, recalling what happened before, took fright and immediately made an effort to walk away. Wyeth caught up and walked with her, causing the girl to burst into tears. He placed both his hands on her shoulders and told her:

"*Don't be frightened.*"

Then, as a prelude to forcing her to the ground, he put his arm around her waist. This time he was unsuccessful and the girl carried on walking while crying her eyes out. Initially, Wyeth walked away from her, but something clicked in his mind. He doubled back and returned to walk menacingly alongside the sobbing girl, causing her even more distress. Why would he do that? What was his motive? Before he could think that far ahead, a friend of the girl came over to them. At this point he separated from the girl and walked ahead on his own. It seemed his interest was only in the little girl when she was unaccompanied.

Wyeth only went as far as the end of the road, where he stopped and waited. A short while later, the little girl came by, again on her own, and again Wyeth walked with her. He again put his hands on her shoulders and told her not to be frightened. Fortunately, that is where the intimidation stopped. Wyeth, perhaps coming to his senses, or not knowing what to do next, finally left the girl for good and continued on his way home. This time, the girl reported what happened and the police caught up with Wyeth. They met him not at his home but instead at the greengrocer's, where, being a minor, his employer, Mr Davies, had to accompany him when he gave a statement to the police. How many similar incidents had gone unreported or Wyeth not been linked with? We may never know. Yet again, Wyeth made a promise:

"*I am very sorry I frightened the little girl and did not know I was doing any harm. I will not speak to any other little girl*".

Although this latest promise to behave lasted longer than his previous statement, Wyeth again could not resist his urge to intimidate unaccompanied young girls. This time he picked up a three-year-old girl, carried her through a hedge and into a field. Wyeth never explained why he, a young man, aged 15-years-old, might have done this, but before he had a chance to do anything a woman entered the field. She grabbed the child from him and carried her away. It seemed Wyeth had a bad reputation with the locals and no one trusted him around little girls. A formal complaint was made to the police which led to Wyeth having to answer for three charges of assault on children and breaching the terms of his probation. The fact he had breached his probation meant he was considered a danger to local children. Therefore, he was not allowed to return home to await his appearance in front of the magistrates. This time he was sent to a 'remand home', by order of the Birmingham Education Office, which saw him spend almost a month at 'Fircourt', Bourneville, in Birmingham. During his time there he acquitted himself well, with records showing he demonstrated a decent level of reading, writing and calculation. His report remarked:

> "*This boy behaved himself quite well, but at the same time I think a year or so on the training ship should make a man of him. He was under medical observation by Dr Auden and he also thought the boy should go to a training ship.*"

Such was Wyeth's reputation locally that, in the lead-up to the court case and while he was on remand, two women came forward and claimed to have seen him acting indecently with a horse. They claimed it happened on 22nd January 1936, and they also claimed to have seen him hanging over the hind legs of the animal while appearing to have sexual intercourse with it. There is nothing on record to indicate why the women did not report it straight away, or why they felt it necessary to wait until Wyeth was due to appear at court to declare it. It is also worth noting that in all the medicals and psychological tests that Wyeth underwent, the reports were constant in saying he did not know much about sexual matters. Perhaps these women were telling the truth. Or perhaps they made it up, seeking to add weight to any sentence handed out, thus keeping Wyeth off their streets longer. Nonetheless their statements never saw the light of day and were certainly not brought before the magistrates.

On 3rd March 1936, with Wyeth accompanied by his probation officer, the Hereford Juvenile Court magistrates had no alternative but to give Wyeth a custodial sentence. He was sent to an approved school, no less than a training ship, as recommended by the remand centre, for a period of up to three years. At least during that time, the little girls living near his parents' home would be safe. It was hoped this intervention would benefit him.

THE TRAINING SHIP, T.S. CORNWALL

The system of 'approved schools' was set up to cater for neglected and delinquent children. Although 15-years-old James Wyeth had left school and was employed, in 1936 he was still regarded as a child, even if it was at the upper age of what was considered childhood. The schools were secure, with children accommodated in basic dormitories. In 1934, the British Government included training ships as being suitable for use as Approved Schools, one of them, Training Ship (T.S.) Cornwall, was berthed at Gravesend, on the River Thames. It was to T.S. Cornwall that Wyeth was sent. The ship was in fact an old wooden frigate battleship, H.M.S. Wellesley, launched and named after the Duke of Wellington in

1815. Its three huge sail masts were a fixture on the Thames since the 1860s, when it retired from active service, moored up and became a training ship for boys aiming to go into the Royal Navy. As an Approved School, the ship was split into three age groups – Junior (10-13), Intermediate (13-15) and Senior (15-17); meaning Wyeth spent the next two years with other lads of his age. But it was far from being a holiday camp. Children detained at T.S. Cornwall were put to hard work and followed a strict naval regime, as laid down by their retired Royal Navy masters. Coincidentally, at the outbreak of war, in 1939, the ship was declassified, and the detainees moved to a camp at High Lodge, Brandon, Suffolk – just a few miles from Thetford.

A file was made on Wyeth during his time on T.S. Cornwall. It noted he was quiet and reserved. When questioned, the he said he was fond of carpentry, reading adventure books, his favourite being Treasure Island, and watching gangster movies. His file noted he stood at 5-foot 6¾-inches tall and weighed 9-stone 6-pounds. The file also documented the fact that, even upon reaching his 16th birthday on the ship, he was still prone to wetting the bed at night and had no knowledge of sexual matters. When he left T.S. Cornwall, in March 1938, an entry in his file stated his conduct had been good. That good behaviour earned him an early release, having served just two years of a three-years sentence. The third year was served at home, while on probation, during which time he reached his 18th birthday, then his actions, should he break the law, would be judged as those of an adult, not as a child. Having earned his early release through good behaviour, his liberty, and no doubt the safety of others, would only be achieved through Wyeth avoiding his previous temptations. Only time would tell.

WYETH'S LAST CHANCE

By the time Wyeth was released, his family had once again moved, this time to 9 Cedar Road, Maidenhead. His mother found him a job at the town's Tesco shop, which back then was more like a traditional grocer than the large supermarket we know today. However, he did not appreciate the banter he received from the female customers. His mother then got him a job with her, packing biscuits at the Weston Biscuit Company's factory in Slough. He started on 16th June 1938 and earned, on average, £4 a week. He found this more to his liking and seemed to do a good enough job, working there for about two years. Two years without any incident being reported. In fact, his manager claimed he was of, "Good general character and conduct."

Then, on 16th April, 1940, a few weeks before his 20th

birthday, Wyeth's malicious side reappeared, this time manifesting into something worse than merely intimidating little girls.

Wyeth was working the night shift at the biscuit factory, from 7pm to 6am, which was long and tiring. After finishing the shift, he began his cycle ride towards home, from Slough to nearby Maidenhead, a distance of about four miles. His shifts were rotated every week, one week it was day shifts, the next it was night shifts. This rotation meant he did not have to work that night, so at the last minute, he decided to take a long detour to visit his aunt who lived in New Haw. The journey was one of about 19 miles long, a journey that took him through Windsor, along the banks of the Thames, over Staines Bridge and onward toward Chertsey.

It was as he was cycling from Staines Bridge to Chertsey, that he overtook a young woman who was cycling in the same direction. After passing her, Wyeth slowed down to such an extent that the woman then had to overtake him. He followed her very closely behind for a few miles until he had to turn off the road and head toward his aunt's home. After having lunch with his aunt, Wyeth then cycled back towards home. He was about five miles into his journey, having just passed through Chertsey, when he stopped to have a cigarette. It was here that he noticed a young woman cycling toward him. He recognised her as being the same person he had overtaken earlier.

As the woman was about to pass, Wyeth stepped into the road and mumbled something to her. She, upon not hearing what he had said, slowed to a stop. By moving closer to understand, she presented herself within Wyeth's reach. He suddenly lunged at her. The woman, being of slight frame, was quickly overpowered, coming off her cycle so violently she hit the ground hard. Such was the swiftness of the attack, she laid stunned for a split second, unable to comprehend what had happened. Not so Wyeth. He immediately reached for her neck, grabbing a tight hold. The woman felt herself being dragged away, by the throat. Then, she was up on her feet, the tight hold around her neck pulling her up, but with her feet barely keeping up with the tempo of her attacker's swift movement. He forced her into a narrow lane, away from the road. She tried to scream, but the grip around her neck stifled any chance of making a noise. Unable to keep her balance, she offered little resistance when she was shoved down into a ditch at the side of the lane. She landed on the soft ground at the bottom. Detecting the grip around her throat had gone, she tried again to scream. However, Wyeth had followed her into the ditch and began punching at the back and side of her head. She also felt blows to her mouth. This was a frenzied attack, one in which Wyeth was trying to silence his victim. Wyeth then proceeded to tie his scarf around her throat and rain down even more punches upon her face. He forced her legs open and laid on top of her. For the first time, she understood what he was saying, as he told her:

"I only want to seduce you, come quietly now."

However, his rapid actions up to that point then stalled. Despite his intent, he was seemingly unsure of what to do next. There was a momentary lull in the violence, as Wyeth simply laid motionless on top of his victim. The woman capitalised upon this inactivity, managing to scream and punch back at Wyeth, who then shouted back:

"I'll knock you out for that."

She screamed again. This time, her blood-curdling scream alerted a passing motorist, who stopped to investigate. The motorist called out. Sensing he would be in trouble if he hung around, Wyeth climbed from the ditch and leapt back onto his cycle, hurriedly travelling back toward Chertsey, although in the opposite direction to his home. In his panic, he realised he had lost a cycle clip in the melee, which would have been left lying in the ditch somewhere. He removed the remaining clip on his other leg and tucked his trousers into his socks to stop them entangling in his cycle chain. Wyeth later told the police the blood on his scarf was when he wiped his injured hand after falling off his cycle, not long after leaving his aunt's home. The reality was, the blood was that of the woman. Her stockings, skirt and coat were stained with that same blood. It later transpired she was 19 years of age, as such she was the only victim who was not vastly younger than him.

Wyeth was asked to attend Weybridge police station, where he was put in an identity line with other men. His victim, accompanied by police officers, then picked him out as the man who assaulted her. Wyeth was taken away to give a statement and true to form, he also offered an apology:

"I don't know what made me do this, something came over me, and I do not know what I was doing, and I am very sorry for what I did to the young lady."

In his statement to the police, Wyeth also claimed to not remember what happened next, but there is no disputing he sexually assaulted her. It was not the first time he could not recall being violent, nor would it be the last.

Initially, his case was heard at Chertsey Petty Sessions, on 17th April, 1940, but due to the seriousness of the crime, and Wyeth's history of offences, it was referred to the Surrey Quarter Sessions, in Kingston upon Thames, where it took place on 21st May, 1940. Wyeth's charge, an "indecent assault on a female, occasioning actual bodily harm", was assessed as that of a young adult and not a child. His mother attended the hearing, acting as a character witness, telling the court her son should be released from the trial so he could join the army. The judge was having none of it, responding that Wyeth's sentence would have to be a custodial one, three years in borstal, a young boys' prison, where "efforts would be made to straighten out the abnormal twist in his nature."

BORSTAL, INMATE NO. 5557

Immediately following Wyeth's sentence, there was some discussion within the borstal system as to where he should be sent. The front-runners were Portland, in Dorset, and Feltham, in Middlesex. The medical officer at Feltham, Dr Rossiter Lewis, suggested Wyeth stay there as Wyeth had spent a week there on remand in the lead-up to the court case. Dr Lewis also stated the court had requested Wyeth have psychological assessments carried out while in borstal, and Dr Lewis had already made some progress on this as preparation for the court case. The Governor of Feltham, also waded in with his support as Feltham being the chosen institution. He noted that Wyeth, during his time on remand there, had a "subnormal intelligence", although was "mentally and physically fit", he also thought Wyeth would benefit from the regime at Feltham. Their arguments were strong enough to sway the authorities, so it was to Feltham that Wyeth was sent.

Initially, Wyeth was unsettled at Feltham, being hostile to other inmates and refusing to communicate. He did slowly settle down, although he remained non-communicative and preferred his own company. Throughout his time there he never socialised or made friends, nor did he co-operate with the psychological assessments that were carried out on him. Dr Lewis, who led Wyeth's treatment, even considered giving up on Wyeth because the offender did not even want to communicate with him. However, the doctor persevered, and it was in December 1940, that he finally got a response from Wyeth. Dr Lewis took this as a sign the borstal regime was working, which raised his hopes of getting more out of Wyeth over the months ahead. However, there was still much work to be done if Dr Lewis was to get to the bottom of Wyeth's mental issues. Just six months later, the authorities reviewed Wyeth's progress in anticipation of releasing him on probation. He had served just a year of his three-year sentence. A document from Feltham, dated 18th June 1941 and in reference to James Wyeth, stated:

"The Institution Board is of the opinion that there is reasonable probability that the above-named Inmate will abstain from crime and lead a useful and industrious life. In accordance with Regulation 12 he is recommended for discharge on licence on the 3rd July 1941."

The borstal authorities accepted the request and exactly a week later, on 25th June, 1941, they granted Wyeth his parole. A statement from a prison doctor, Dr Caudwell, referred to Wyeth's behaviour. How much contact this doctor had with Wyeth is not known, but his statement read:

"This lad was discharged on 26.6.41 after every aspect of the case had been considered. His general conduct here had been satisfactory and he proved to be an excellent worker. Prior to discharge he had been mixing better with other lads and forming friendships which were above suspicion. It was very difficult, however, to gain this lad's confidence on sexual matters and the outlook for him in this respect is uncertain. His intelligence was below normal but not enough to render him liable to certification under the Mental Deficiency Acts, on this occasion. I found no evidence of a psychosis."

In response, Dr Lewis wrote to the authorities, warning them that Wyeth may re-offend.

"Psychological treatment has not, in this case, met with acceptance; the general control exercised in the Borstal

Institution appears to have had a stabilising effect however. No question of mental deficiency or insanity has been raised during his period of training.

During the last two months a lack of proper self-control had been noticed on occasions and has taken the form of bullying.

The prognosis is uncertain and a recrudescence of assault tactics at some future date is not unlikely."

Dr Lewis' warning that Wyeth my re-offend was backed up by a comment handwritten on Wyeth's borstal file. It was unsigned, so we will never know who, or how qualified, the person was who wrote it.

"He should remain at Feltham and call for further report in 3 months."

Dr Lewis' assessment and the stark warning notwithstanding, Wyeth was allowed back home with his parents, although once again under licence. His liberty was subject to him reporting regularly to his parole officer and leading a life free from crime. The latter was something he had not been able to adhere to, following previous misdemeanours. He was given a parole number – B.11844; and his licence was valid for almost three years, to expire on 20th May, 1944. Any breach to the conditions of his licence meant Wyeth would be returned immediately to custody. Had the authorities considered the weight of Dr Lewis' assessment, then Wyeth may not have been released early and Pat would have been safe. So, why did the authorities release him after he had served only a third of his sentence and while there were doubts about his future conduct? To answer this, we must reflect upon the world during that time. Great Britain was at war and needed every available man, who was able to fight, to join the Armed Forces. Wyeth's medical report stated he was mentally and physically fit, thus making him a prime candidate to enlist, rather than dwell inside borstal. Wyeth's mother had pleaded with the magistrates at his last court case to allow him to go into the army instead of prison. It also seemed Wyeth had made a promise to enlist as soon as he could. The Army was even mentioned in the review of his parole application.

"Home to Maidenhead, before joining the Army. He is of age for military service."

As one of the conditions of his parole Wyeth should have been compelled to report to the Aylesbury After-Care Association. However, two weeks after his release, this became irrelevant, when Wyeth went to Birmingham and enlisted into the Army. From that point on, he had no parole officer to report to, no doctor conducting psychological assessments on him and, as a soldier, a new start where no one knew his past.

There is a slight 'hiccup' to the release of Chief Inspector Barratt's thorough report. Captain Stephen Van Neck, Chief Constable of Norfolk County Constabulary, is not happy to have received his copy after the Director of Public Prosecutions (DPP) and New Scotland Yard got theirs. In his experience, it is usual for the 'host' police force, in this case Norfolk, to submit the report to the DDP. After all, Norfolk police began investigating the attack before Barratt arrived at Thetford railway station, so he feels he should have been given the opportunity to add input from his force. What actually happened was, Barratt simultaneously released it to the DPP, his own boss at New Scotland Yard and Captain Van Neck. For some reason, Van Neck's copy was delayed in transit. Nonetheless, the chief constable is none too pleased, so he writes to the DPP. at Piccadilly, London, W1.

"I understand that Chief Inspector Barratt of New Scotland Yard has forwarded to you a history of the case, together with statements, etc. This is an irregular proceeding, as these papers should have been forwarded from this office in the usual way. There seems to have been a muddle due to the fact that Detective Garner, who handled the case as far as the Norfolk Constabulary was concerned, went sick directly after the investigations were completed."

Despite Garner going sick after the investigation, Van Neck still holds him accountable, feeling the detective should have advised Barratt of the correct process.

SATURDAY, 30ᵀᴴ MAY, 1942

On headed paper – "Chief Constable's Office, County Constabulary, Norwich"; Captain Stephen Van Neck, in a frank handwritten letter to New Scotland Yard, shows how upset he is with Barratt about the mix up, although he graciously mentions the detective did work very hard on the investigation.

"Many thanks for the copy of the police report in the Wyeth case. I was a bit fed up with Chief Inspector Barratt in dashing off without coming to see me and taking the case direct to the Director of Public Prosecutions before I had a chance to see it and I wrote and told the Commissioner so. In the last murder case in which we called upon you, Chief Inspector Bridger discussed procedure with me, and I wrote to the Director and told him I had arranged with Bridger for a copy of the file to be taken to him. I don't know what your orders are but no Chief Constable likes to have Scotland Yard coming in and "bouncing" him in this way. It's bad for the discipline of my C.I.D. – a department which has to be handled pretty firmly or they get above themselves. Thank God I am not responsible for your C.I.D.! But I can't think they are encouraged to be so discourteous.

Both Barratt and Detective Sergeant Webb worked like horses and so did my chaps and they all got on extremely well together. I gave Barratt all the facilities he asked for including an extra telephone line put in to Thetford Police Station. The report on the case is excellent – now I have been allowed to see it!!

Yours sincerely,

Stephen Van Neck

P.S. London seems a safer place than Norwich these days. We are too damned near to the East Coast and get disturbed by every wandering Hun coming and going. Hope you are well."

Van Neck's comment that Norwich did not feel very safe reminds us the war was still very much a mortal threat to daily life. In April, May and June 1942, Norwich was subjected to aerial bombing from the German Luftwaffe as part of the 'Baedeker Raids', when the enemy concentrated their efforts on cities of historical importance. As well as Norwich; Bath, Canterbury, Exeter and York were also targeted. Of the 35,000 homes in Norwich, 2,000 were destroyed, 27,000 more were damaged and fewer than 5,000 escaped unscathed. 222 people lost their lives and countless others were injured. Throughout all this destruction the Norfolk County Constabulary continued to oversee routine law and order, while ensuring enough police were able to investigate serious crime. A point worth considering if we are to understand their limitations in investigating Pat's murder.

MONDAY, 1ST JUNE, 1942

Captain Van Neck receives a reply to his complaint, although perhaps not the answer he was hoping for. Sir Norman Kendal, C.B.E., Assistant Commissioner of New Scotland Yard, writes back under the heading, 'Personal and Confidential'. Sir Norman clears up the confusion by saying the report was released simultaneously and, unfortunately, Van Neck's copy was somehow delayed. Also, any New Scotland Yard officer leading an investigation outside of London, would usually be expected to create their report in the capital and release it from there, but Barratt, leading his first case outside London, released his report while in Norfolk. It was merely an error on that account and nothing intended.

Van Neck responds, on more than one occasion, over the next few days, still venting his frustration. He comments that he is not impressed that one of his own typists had to type up the report, when Sir Norman confirms it should have been done in London. He also feels Barratt had not conferred with him enough through all the stages of the investigation. However, he does finally concede the report was for New Scotland Yard to submit. In his last letter to Sir Norman, Van Neck goes on to commend Barratt and Webb.

"I don't want Barratt to get any 'black marks' because he and Sergeant Webb worked extremely hard and most efficiently, and got on very well with my men. I propose, when the case is finished, to write officially to say how well these two officers did."

This is a promise Van Neck does in fact keep. He also admits he may not have handled the situation well.

"I expect you will give Barratt a quiet tip before he is sent on another County case, that County Chief Constables are inclined to be a bit touchy!!"

EAST HARLING POLICE STATION, NORFOLK
THURSDAY, 4TH JUNE, 1942

On Monday, 1st June, 1942, James Wyeth was brought from Norwich prison to attend a hearing before the Justices at East Harling Petty Sessions. That hearing was adjourned until today – Thursday, 4th June – after Detective Inspector Garner requested a delay. While at the hearing, Wyeth was granted legal aid to assist him with the costs of his defence. Wyeth was then returned to Norwich until his return to East Harling.

East Harling's police station, hosting the courtroom, looks nothing more than a red brick townhouse in the centre of the village. It is set among similar looking red brick buildings and, just a few yards away, a war memorial is located inside a tiny park. Such a setting in this sleepy village belies the fact it is taking part in what could be one of the most notorious crimes of the year. Today, in what will be the first glimpse of how Wyeth's court case will pan out, Justice Colonel Edward Mornement, aged 72, is chairing the bench. Mornement owns a dredging company and lives in a large house in East Harling. He will be assisted by two other local magistrates – Noah Barker, a 75-year-old dairy farmer, and 65-year-old Harlan T. Phoenix, a secretary of the local Friendly Society. They are more used to deciding on cases of theft or breaking the 'black-out' wartime restrictions, than a high-profile child murder case.

Leading the prosecution is Mr Gerald Paling, a solicitor representing the Director of Public Prosecutions. He first outlines the horrific injuries inflicted upon Pat. Then, reading out Chief Inspector Barratt's report, he repeats Wyeth's statements made at Thetford police station. Next, 20 statements are presented to the room, including those from Mr and Mrs Pask, forensics, soldiers and police. Dr Webster, the Home Office pathologist, has his report read out to the room. This is intense. There are more forensic reports, specifically the fibres and blood found on Wyeth's clothing. Lastly, Detective Sergeant Webb stands before the room saying he was present when Wyeth was at Thetford and admitted to Chief Inspector Barratt about attacking Pat, and then when they all went on to Riddlesworth Park, where Wyeth showed them how he approached Pat. It is a lengthy hearing, although worth noting all this evidence pertains to the prosecution of Wyeth, not for his defence. Arrangements have already been made to reconvene tomorrow, should there be a need for extra time to hear all the evidence that will be presented.

Colonel Mornement then addresses Wyeth:

"Do you wish to say anything in answer to the charge?

You are not obliged to say anything unless you desire to do so; but whatever you say will be taken down in writing, and may be given in evidence upon your trial."

Mornement knows this will go one of two ways. Either Wyeth will accept the charge of murder and declare himself guilty, or he will plead not guilty. If it is the latter, then Mornement will need to refer the case to a higher court, where there will be complicated defence and prosecution arguments to be heard. Although Wyeth has already confessed to the murder, he is now receiving legal advice by his defence counsel, led by Frank Theodore Alpe, a native of Norfolk, and Mr Montague Philip Solomon. Both are experienced barristers and have been briefed by Wyeth's solicitors – Greenland Houchen & Co., 16 Bank Street, Norwich, Norfolk. They advise Wyeth on his response.

"I am not guilty."

Wyeth is informed he can bring his own defence witnesses to the courtroom and even defend himself against the allegation of murder if he so wishes, to which he replies:

"I reserve my defence."

Wyeth's responses mean the case is now beyond the remit of Mornement and the East Harling magistrates, so the legal proceedings against Wyeth will now take place in a higher court, that of the Central Criminal Court, in London, otherwise known as the 'Old Bailey'. A provisional trial date is set for Tuesday, 23rd June, 1942. Wyeth's indictment reads:

"That he did, on the 5th May, 1942, at Riddlesworth Park, in the County of Norfolk, murder Patricia Ann Cupit. (Against the Peace)"

TUESDAY, 9TH JUNE, 1942

The DPP nominates its barristers. They are the newly knighted Sir Charles Doughty and Mr Gerald Howard. Sir Charles earned the King's Counsel in 1925, meaning he is one of the most experienced and capable lawyers in the capital, if not the nation. Coincidentally, Mr Howard's roots are in West Suffolk, which encapsulates Riddlesworth.

THURSDAY, 11TH JUNE, 1942

Dr Henry Smith Holden, who conducted the forensic report into Pat's and Wyeth's clothing, writes to the DPP asking that the court case be put back, citing he is already booked to appear at other court cases. With less than two weeks to go, he doubts he will be free to attend Wyeth's trial, so he suggests a date, sometime in July. Gerald Paling, replying on behalf of the DPP, says he will see what he can do, but cannot promise anything as it is getting near to the court date.

TUESDAY, 16TH JUNE, 1942

Wyeth is transferred to Brixton prison. The primary reason is the doctor who became familiar with the prisoner's medical history, while he was held there a couple of years ago, can carry out further psychological assessments if he is brought to him. The governor of Norwich prison questions this move, in relation to how it will affect access to Wyeth by the defence team, who are based in Norwich. The team of solicitors, Greenland Houchen & Co., respond by saying they have no urgent plans to see him, so they agree to the move. There is however a stipulation made on Wyeth's prison record by the governor. It is that, should he be found guilty of murder, which is a capital crime, then he is to be returned to Norwich prison, where the sentence of death by hanging, will be carried out.

WEDNESDAY, 17TH JUNE, 1942

Greenland, Houchen & Co., the Norwich-based solicitors acting on behalf of Wyeth, also write to the DPP to request a delay to the upcoming court case. It seems they are struggling to collate, and indeed receive, all the information they need from their sources across the country. Sites in Pembroke, Carmarthen, London, Hereford, and many other places, have been contacted regarding Wyeth's history and the solicitors need to put information into some order before then passing it over to Frank Alpe, the Defence Counsel. In fact, they claim they are still waiting on a report from a doctor who has been psychologically assessing Wyeth at Brixton, which is key to their defence. The report is due on Monday, 22nd June, so with the trial booked for the day after, they will not be in full possession of the facts from that report. They suggest the case is put back to no sooner than 14th July. The reply from the DPP is that any decision to postpone the court is purely a matter for the judge sitting on the case and not for anyone else.

Later, the Lord Chief Justice, sitting in the Old Bailey, listens to the defence reasons for delaying the trial. Also present are Chief Inspector Barratt and the solicitors for the prosecution, with the latter offering no objection to the delay. The judge decides in favour of giving the defence more time. The trial is postponed for three weeks.

THE HOME SECRETARY INTERVENES
MONDAY, 29TH JUNE, 1942

If there is any proof needed that those in the upper echelons of power were taking an interest in Wyeth's case, then it was provided by this sudden mandate, made by none other than Winston Churchill's Home Secretary, Herbert Morrison.

"To the Governor of His Majesty's Prison at Brixton and all others whom it may concern.

By virtue of the powers vested in me by Section 11 of the Prison Act, 1898, I hereby order that James Wyeth, Register Number 4350, a prisoner in your custody, be produced at the Mental Hospital, Runwell, Chelmsford, on Wednesday the 1st July, 1942, at 3p.m. and at such time and place thereafter as may be necessary, to undergo a medical examination.

(Signed) Herbert Morrison"

The piece of law Morrison refers to gives him explicit authority to intervene. Here is that part from Section 11,

"Section 11.(1) A Secretary of State, on proof to his satisfaction that the presence of any prisoner at any place is required in the interest of justice, or for the purpose of any public inquiry, may by writing under his hand order that the prisoner be taken to that place."

It is worth noting it is Wyeth's defence lawyers who

have petitioned the Home Secretary for the test to take place, which will prove significant later when, despite all the legal arguments, forensic evidence and witness statements presented at court, it will be the Secretary of State, from his office in Whitehall, who will have the final say on Wyeth's fate.

WEDNESDAY 1ST JULY, 1942

Today, Wyeth is taken from Brixton prison to Runwell Hospital, where the brain specialists will use a ground breaking piece of equipment, called an encephalograph. This involves the placing of electrodes on the patient's scalp to detect electrical pulses within the brain. The equipment is so state-of-the-art, that this is the first time ever it is being used in a murder trial. Wyeth's defence team wishes to prove that he has an abnormality in his brain, maybe epilepsy. This, they hope, will explain the reason he claims to not remember attacking Pat.

MEDICAL REPORTS

TUESDAY, 14TH JULY, 1942

Dr Rossiter Lewis assessed Wyeth after the accused was sent to Feltham borstal, a couple of years ago. Now Dr Lewis, following a request from the defence solicitors, has released his report he made on Wyeth from that time. In the report, Dr Lewis confirms he first saw Wyeth in April 1940. He routinely runs health checks over new inmates, and with Wyeth he learned the young man had suffered sunstroke when he young. This seemed severe enough for him to have suffered a fever and headaches, with long-lasting symptoms akin to encephalitis lethargica, otherwise known as the 'sleeping sickness'. The illness affects the brain, sometimes leaving victims in, even if just temporarily, a speechless and motionless state. Despite this, Wyeth had not presented himself as someone who was, according to the 1940s classification, insane. However, the report noted 20-year-old Wyeth's mental age was comparable to that of an 11-year-old. He did appear, after time, to mix with other inmates but was prone to bullying some of those who were younger than him. Other than that, he came across as a reliable hard worker.

Dr Lewis would routinely, and regularly, interview Wyeth about his past actions. The doctor claims to have never witnessed Wyeth talk openly about any sexual activity, nor received reports about Wyeth doing so, during his time in borstal. However, the doctor does have a theory as to why Wyeth may have attacked the young woman who was cycling near Chertsey. He noted:

"... one feature of the case which might have been of importance in explaining his conduct (namely, assaulting a young woman) was that his first heterosexual experience had been said by him to have occurred as a result of invitation from an older person, when he was only 8 years of age. It was suggested that the fact that he was of low intelligence and had little power to control his desires for sexual indulgence had led to the rather primitive attempt of gaining an introduction to a member of the opposite sex by forcing company on her, and that it had gone further than this in that an actual assault – undoubtedly for sexual purposes – had also occurred."

When it looked likely Wyeth was going to be released on probation early, Dr Lewis changed tact and suggested coping mechanisms for Wyeth, to help him upon his release. In referring to this, the medical officer said he felt Wyeth's psychotherapy was carried out as effectively as possible, but it was rushed and never felt satisfactory.

"During the whole of his twelve months at Feltham Institution I was never able to contact the 'real' Wyeth. He would not speak openly or say more than a few words, never

enter into any kind of discussion, and when interviewed always remained morose and secretive.

I came to regard him towards the end of the first twelve months as a person of psychopathic personality with no signs or symptoms of certifiable mental disorder, but one for whom the best course would have been a prolonged period in borstal.

He proved resistant to suggestion and to ordinary psychotherapy."

EVELYN'S JIM

There is a need to understand James Wyeth's personal history, especially how his upbringing may have affected his subsequent mental health. The police have done well so far, detailing Wyeth's past interactions with the judicial system and uncovering some basic details of his life, most of the latter gleaned from his adoptive mother, Evelyn. The police, however, are seen as being very formal. They are invariably male and arrive in uniform or, in the case of detectives, a formal suit and tie, whereupon they jot down notes before requiring a signed statement. Another tactic, to delve deeper into Wyeth's past, takes the form of a softer approach. Social services do not require a signed statement, but instead are more likely to pop round to chat with Evelyn over a cup of tea. The two social workers assigned to speak with Evelyn are women, who can relate more to Evelyn's emotions, especially as they are very experienced in their respective fields. Mrs Beach has spent many years supervising ex-inmates released from Broadmoor and currently works for the Central Association for Mental Welfare, while Mrs D.H. Hardcastle was formerly Chief Psychiatric Social Worker at the Department of Psychological Medicine at Guy's Hospital, but is now Organiser of Social Workers for the Mental Health Emergency Committee. They are also experienced enough to know they cannot lead Evelyn's answers or influence her in any way. Evelyn must feel comfortable enough to offer what she sees to be true, rather than tell the social workers what she believes they want to hear.

Evelyn, in her discussions with the social workers, refers to her son as "Jim". While there can be no justification for Wyeth's actions, indeed Evelyn makes no effort to defend the actions of her son, it is an undeniable fact that the love Evelyn has for her son has remained steadfast throughout his life. She is also the only person to stand by him, no matter what he has done, always trying to keep him on the right track, even if that meant finding him a job. She is the only person who can relay to us some level of humanity for an otherwise very troubled individual. To that end, Evelyn requires nothing but praise for all her efforts. The following paragraphs describe what the social workers were told, through the eyes of Evelyn. In an attempt to convey her love for her son, to give a view through the eyes of Evelyn, Wyeth will be referred to as "Jim" for the next few paragraphs.

The two social workers knock at the door of 9 Cedars Road, Maidenhead, the Wyeths' family home, and are let in by Evelyn, who is just three weeks away from her forty-fourth birthday. Evelyn's mother recently passed away and she has had to deal with the funeral, while trying to avoid the gossip about her son. Yet, despite her loss, she is determined to deal with the trauma of her adopted son's murder charge, although she will bear this burden alone. Her husband has distanced himself from their adopted son, to the extent of quitting his printing job to find new employment where he hopes no one will associate him with the child murderer. If truth be told, Mr Wyeth has never really taken to his adopted son at all.

Evelyn gave birth when she and her husband were living in Rhydyfelin, Glamorgan, but sadly the baby died soon after, leaving her heartbroken. When she saw a newspaper advertisement, by the NSPCC, for someone to come forward and adopt a baby boy, she jumped in with both feet first. She did discuss this with her husband although he was firmly against it, nonetheless she made enquiries. The response from the authorities was that the baby was a bonny little boy who had received a bad upbringing and was simply looking for a loving mother. For Evelyn, it seemed the perfect match, so she told the authorities she was very much interested in taking on the boy as her own. However, as Evelyn readily admits, the first time she clapped eyes on her new son, she was left feeling utterly disappointed. He was far from being a bonny little boy, but instead she described him as being a thin miserable specimen. It was too late to change anything though, emotionally she had already begun to bond with him. Come what may, through thick and thin, in her eyes, Jim was now her son.

At this point it is worth knowing the circumstances leading to Jim being adopted. His natural mother, Kathleen Crane, was one of nine children, whose father was a poorly paid farm worker. Kathleen's mother died a year after giving birth to her, leaving the children to more or less fend for themselves while their father and older children went to work. Concerned local residents, seeing the family's poverty, even raised collections of money and clothing to help them out. This upbringing impacted on Kathleen. In 1914, while still being of school age, she was convicted of "larceny of money" and sent to an 'Industrial School'. Such schools had been introduced to provide homeless, poor and neglected children, under the age of 14, a state-run education. Some were boarding schools, while others were day schools, often run within a strict regime. The idea was to offer the children basic life-skills, including moral guidance, religion, housework, but could also include learning a trade, such as tailoring and gardening. However, magistrates did often direct unruly children from poor families to them as a form of punishment. These schools were reformed after the Great War and became known as 'Approved Schools'. It is probably no coincidence that Kathleen's son was destined to spend time at one. Upon her release she appears to have led a traveller's lifestyle, often leading to accusations of vagrancy. Indeed, only in the past few days have the police managed to track her down to Carmarthenshire, where she is living with travellers. The police report states she has a below average mental age, and is dirty and unkempt.

Kathleen informed the police that her son, James Thomas Crane, was born in Priory Mount, near Haverfordwest, but she did not know who the father was, although she suspected he worked on a farm where she was once employed. When her son was aged about 10-months-old, she began living a traveller's lifestyle, taking him with her. She then went on to have another baby, a daughter. On 10th October 1921, Kathleen was sentenced to a day's imprisonment for child neglect and her children put up for adoption. It was then, that Evelyn Wyeth applied to adopt the boy. Kathleen's daughter has since become institutionalised on account of epilepsy and there are no plans for her release. The police report that Kathleen's sister, Alice, is also institutionalised at Maghull Institution, in Liverpool.

When Evelyn first brought Jim home all he did was scream. It seemed he screamed through the night, screamed through the day, and should he be pacified and content, then the second anyone approached him, well, he screamed in fright. A few months later a doctor diagnosed Jim as having a tubercular condition of the bowel. The doctor then instructed Evelyn to take the child back to the NSPCC because the condition would most likely affect him for the rest of his life. She had none of it, instead, feeling she had a commitment to both her son and the NSPCC to raise Jim as she would her own son, she nursed him back to good health.

In all aspects, Jim was a very late developer. He did not start talking until aged three and could not walk until he was four. Evelyn struggled to get Jim toilet trained, and even as an adult he still occasionally wets the bed. As a child he would often complain of headaches, saying, "Don't talk. My head hurts".

Jim would then be seen banging his head in an effort to cure his headache. Evelyn thought he looked like an old grandmother when he rocked back and forwards during his bouts of headaches. Despite doing all she could for him, his condition was not helped when, at the age of six, he got sunstroke, resulting in a high temperature and him screaming so loud the neighbours complained. During this episode, Jim suffered hallucinations, such as seeing rats climbing the walls. Evelyn, as ever, was by his side throughout this, despite by then having another son, this time one she gave birth to. Derrick Wyeth is five years younger than Jim.

Jim went to the local school in Rhydyfelin, and apparently the headmaster once described Jim as being, "a good boy, but could not learn". By all accounts Jim was extremely solitary and never mixed with the other children or played with toys at school. At home, if anyone gave him a toy, he would promptly wrap it up and put it away. Either that, or set about destroying it. Even his hobbies were solitary ones, such as woodwork and gardening. Yet, even in his own garden, he would spook the neighbours. On one occasion, a neighbour was spring cleaning, regularly popping out of her home to shake rugs and bring out rubbish. The task took her about five hours to complete, throughout which, she observed Jim was stood in his garden, in the same location and position, just staring ahead. Five hours of no movement, just staring at nothing in particular. Jim was always reluctant to go out with the family, for example on picnics and to the cinema, instead preferring to stay home. Evelyn and her husband would return and find Jim still sat in exactly the same position that they left him. Evelyn often felt Jim looked upon her and her husband with some disdain, nonetheless she persevered trying to bring him out of his 'shell'. When Jim left school, Evelyn urged her son to go to the local Y.M.C.A. to play darts with people of his own age, but he soon came home, telling her no one would speak to him. Evelyn knew the instructor and asked him about this. He confirmed there was no interaction between Jim and the lads. The reason it seemed was that one or two of them had indeed tried to initiate a conversation, but it was Jim who blanked them. He also made the other lads feel uncomfortable, so there was no love lost when he left and did not return. Evelyn does confess that Jim very often tried her patience too. He would sit at home, never initiating conversation, barely answering anyone else, simply sitting there for hours just staring at nothing. There were times she felt like screaming, it got on her nerves, but still she persisted.

Jim left school, aged 15, poorly qualified and, due to strained finances of his family, with no prospect of further education. Being brought up in Wales, there was pressure on him to seek employment in the coal mines, but Evelyn did not want this, so she got him a job as a houseboy in a local hotel. The job involved general cleaning, laundry, ironing and taking out the rubbish, but in hindsight Evelyn felt her son did too many little odd jobs rather than learn a specific role, which didn't help him. She felt he needed structure. She also thought the description of the place as a hotel was misleading, for she felt it was nothing more than a tea room. However, this was the place, in 1935, where Jim first fell foul of the law. Next door to the hotel was a farm and one day the farmer's young daughter was outside playing. Whether it was due to a lack of structure, or something else, is debatable, nonetheless Jim popped across to the girl and attacked her. Evelyn mentions Jim's attacks on girls, but glosses over the details.

There was no chance Jim could carry on working at the hotel, so Evelyn got him a job as an errand boy in a greengrocer shop in Hereford. However, it was not long before he got in trouble again for assaulting little girls, leading to his appearance before the Hereford Juvenile Court. Following the latest misdemeanour, a doctor at Hereford Hospital requested to treat Jim for certain mental health disorders, but the authorities deemed it better that Jim was punished for his crimes, so they sent him to the training ship, T.S. Cornwall. Evelyn felt, despite the offer of a doctor to look at her son's mental health, Jim seemed happy and responded well to the discipline on the ship. He even won a medal for running cross country. Up to that point, it was unheard of for Jim to have received such recognition for something he had done well. Upon finishing his time on T.S. Cornwall, he was released back to his parents, who by then had again moved house, this time to Maidenhead.

Evelyn found him another job, again working in a local greengrocer shop, but this did not work well. Jim had developed into a young man by then, with a good physique, yet he was still socially isolated with little interest in the opposite sex. Therefore, when female customers visited the shop and gave Jim 'banter', he could not cope and became very depressed. He left the shop and Evelyn, who was working at the newly opened Weston Biscuit Factory, in nearby Slough, got him a job with her. He seemed to progress well there, and became a valued worker, but then another incident of assault on a young woman saw him convicted and sent to borstal. Evelyn regularly visited him during his time at Feltham, although Jim rarely ever talked during her visits, nor would he accept any gifts of fruit and sweets that she offered him. Nonetheless, and unperturbed by the lack of response from her son, she persisted with visiting him throughout his time there. Apart from legal and medical representatives, Evelyn was the only person to visit Jim while he was held on remand. If she could not visit, then she sent him cigarettes through the post. On the rare occasions he did talk, he would say he had plenty to eat and he was happy. When they spoke of what he would do once he had served his time, he seemed sad to leave the strict discipline of the borstal regime and spoke of joining the army as an infantry soldier. In 1941, he left borstal and did just that, enlisting with the army, but was posted to the Pioneers Corps, which he did not appreciate. Their main tasks were labouring, digging and guarding bases, far from the heroics of the infantry that Jim imagined himself being involved with. Nonetheless, according to Evelyn, he went without any fuss.

Evelyn does not believe Jim has had any proper relationships with girls. The nearest he came was when he was just over fifteen-years-old and became friends with a girl of a similar age. The term 'friends' must be used loosely because when the two of them went for walks, Jim would rarely speak or offer any affection. When the girl's mother found out about the relationship, she put an immediate stop to it and banned her daughter from seeing him again. Jim did not appear too bothered by this and did not appear to miss the 'friendship' either. This was in stark contrast to Evelyn's other son, Derrick, who grew up playing with friends, sometimes getting up to mischief and lately developing a healthy interest in girls.

Nonetheless, the determined Evelyn says she will stand, singularly and steadfastly, by her son Jim, even though his name is being reported in national and regional newspapers across this nation. However, the murder case has tested even her resolve. Evelyn will not openly admit it, but she hints to the social workers that perhaps Jim would have been much happier growing up in, as she terms it, "a Mental Home", rather than the life he has had with her. His name, for now, is easily recognisable to most of Britain, which prompts her to request if the two social workers can do anything to have

Jim tried under his natural surname of Crane, instead of her family name of Wyeth. Poor Evelyn, it seems, is feeling the strain.

AN UNLIKELY ALLY

The magistrates who deliberated on Wyeth, in the Juvenile Courts of 1935 and 1936, after he was accused of attacking little girls, want their input into his imminent trial at the Old Bailey. They formulate a letter with their Clerk of the Court and hand it in at Hereford Police Station. The letter is then passed to the Chief Constable of the City of Hereford Police, who in turn posts it to Chief Inspector Thomas Barratt. It seems the Hereford magistrates, although offering no evidence for the trial itself, have instead some mitigating circumstances they feel need to be considered if Wyeth is found guilty. They know Wyeth could face the death penalty, so they feel the judge needs to see their letter before deciding upon any sentence. In fact, their words echo some of what Evelyn Wyeth has told the two social workers.

"Dear Sir.

In the event of James Wyeth being convicted of murder, we, the magistrates of the Juvenile Court before whom he appeared on various occasions at the age of 15, would be glad if this letter might be shown to the Judge.

The charge against the boy at that time was always the same, assaulting little girls, but though he took them off for long solitary walks, he did not frighten them or, as far as we could find out, touch them at all. In every other way the boy's character was good.

We were informed that, as a baby, he had been subjected to some dreadful ill-treatment and, whether because of this, or not, we were convinced that there existed some impulse which was quite beyond his control and which was potentially of extreme danger to himself and the public.

We felt that this was a case for the most skilled psychological treatment we could procure; we therefore sent him to the Remand Home in Birmingham with the request that he should attend the Child Guidance Clinic from there. There being no boarding facilities at the clinic, he was kept for some weeks at the Remand Home, but when he returned we were told he had not been to the clinic at all, the authorities 'not having considered it necessary'. We had no power to enforce our wishes, so, the offences recurring, we had to send him to an approved school; we felt, however, at the time that, through no fault of his own he had been denied the one course which might possibly have saved him.

The impression he has left on our minds is of a rather gentle shy boy, bewildered and frightened by the recurrence of an impulse which he did not understand, and it is because we feel that our knowledge at that time may be of some very slight assistance now, that we are presuming to write this letter."

Just in the nick of time, with the trial beginning tomorrow, Dr Hugh Grierson releases his medical report to the Director of Public Prosecutions. So late is the report's release that the defence will have little, if any, time to react. Mind you, you can sense frustration in Grierson's report when he alleges the defence did not tell him the result of the test ordered by the Home Secretary. Grierson has had access to Wyeth, at Brixton prison, for the past month. He has also received reports from prison officers about the accused's conduct and read the various police reports on the prisoner. He begins his report with the family history of Wyeth, including the prisoner's sister and aunt being institutionalised through mental health issues. The report then goes on:

"I have obtained no history of fits or insanity in the accused himself. According to reports, his foster mother states the lad was not quite normal and that his general demeanour has drawn comments from the neighbours.

On 25.6.42 he was seen and examined for the defence by Dr Louis Rose. Dr Rose did not discuss the case with me after his examination, but on 1.7.42 the accused was sent to Runwell Hospital, on the application of defending solicitors, for examination by the electro-encephalograph. What the result of this examination was, I do not know, for I have not been informed. In view of this, on 14th July, 1942, the accused was sent to the Sutton Emergency Hospital and an electro-encephalograph record was there taken by Dr J.D.N. Hill, who reports as follows:

"This E.E.G. shows non-specific abnormalities in minor degrees. They indicate a predisposition to a group of disorders of which epilepsy is the commonest. They are found in a high percentage of the relatives of epileptics. It is not possible from this E.E.G. to say definitely whether Wyeth suffers or has at any time suffered from epilepsy."

Whilst under my care he has eaten and slept normally; in the ward he has kept mostly to himself, reading, and had little to do with other inmates. At interviews he has shown mostly a passive attitude, being a person of few words and usually speaking only when spoken to. This attitude is, I think, due to an introverted state rather than to indolence. He stated that he had 'black-out' or 'black-fits' in the past but when examined on these I could obtain no definite instances. All he would say was that he forgot for a time where he was when he brooded at home.

His past history of assaults on girls is in line with the present charge, and I notice that in 1940, when convicted on his own plea of such an assault, he alleged that he did not remember all that had happened. He now states that his memory returned later.

As to the present charge, he repeats what he has already said to the police, that is, that he does not remember what happened after dragging the girl under the trees. The period this alleged loss of memory covers is that in which the alleged murder was supposedly committed. Beyond his own statement I find no further evidence of any mental disease or disorder with which a loss of memory might be associated. I have subjected this to intelligence tests and find this to be practically normal.

In conclusion, he is a person of the introverted and solitary type. I am not satisfied that his alleged loss of memory is genuine and I have not found signs of any mental disease which would, in my opinion, prevent him from knowing what he was doing or that when he did was wrong.

He is fit to plead to the indictment.

I have the honour to be, Sir, Your obedient servant,

(Sgd) Hugh A Grierson, M.B. B.B. Lond., Senior Medical Officer."

Dr Grierson's report is now the final piece of the evidence jigsaw before the trial begins. Over the past two months, it became apparent that the defence were not going to question the accusation of their client attacking Pat. Indeed, the defence have not supplied anyone who can provide their client with an alibi and, in any case, Wyeth readily confessed to the crime. Instead, all enquiries point to the trial being a battle over Wyeth's state of mind. The general feeling among experts is that he is currently of sound mind and should stand for trial, but they differ upon whether he was in control of that mind when he attacked Pat. Is she a victim of Wyeth's psychosis rather than Wyeth himself? At the conclusion of the trial, it will ultimately be the jury and judge who decides whether Wyeth faces being suspended from the hangman's noose.

PART THREE – THE TRIAL
THURSDAY, 16TH JULY, 1942

The Central Criminal Court of England and Wales, better known as the Old Bailey, has not been immune to the ravages of war. During the Blitz, when the Luftwaffe concentrated its attacks on London, parts of the court's outer walls collapsed after receiving direct hits. Until recently, workmen and cranes were still working on the site, clearing away rubble and making temporary repairs. However, large gaping holes remain. Although the mortal threat of aerial bombing has diminished since the Blitz, the Old Bailey serves throughout, as an ever-present reminder that justice continues, no matter what happens outside. Despite all the death and destruction across the world, those brought before the judges remain accountable for their actions. Notwithstanding any unforeseen air raid sirens today, the trial of James Wyeth is to begin, and should conclude tomorrow. The courtroom has not been booked for a day longer. Wyeth is accused of a capital crime, meaning within 48 hours he could learn his life is to be ended by the hangman's noose. Ominously for him, especially in consideration of his alleged crime, above the main entrance to the court building, sculptured in stone, are the words, "DEFEND THE CHILDREN OF THE POOR AND PUNISH THE WRONGDOER."

Inside the building, the courtroom for Wyeth's hearing presents a formal setting. The walls are wood-panelled. Low-walled booths, to segregate the judge, court officials, lawyers and the public gallery, are also wood-panelled. The room offers an air of stateliness, to which the barristers and court officials will be familiar with, but the wrongdoers may well find this unfamiliar and quite daunting. But then, this is the judge's domain. The judge's 'throne' – a leather upholstered high back chair elevated above the proceedings, from where they issue their commands – is positioned at one end of the courtroom, behind a wood-panelled desk. The judge for Wyeth's case is 62-year-old Justice Frederic Wrottesley, a highly experienced judge, who became King's Counsel 16 years ago. Wrottesley has also written books about the law and the examination of witnesses, books which are the suggested reading matter for those entering into the profession. In 1937 he was knighted by the King and, among his peers, Wrottesley is one of the most highly respected judges in the land.

Wrottesley heads for his chair. From his vantage point, he sees the clerk of the court directly below him, also behind wood panelling. The clerk will ensure the proceedings run smoothly. He has already prepared evidence into the order it will be called, made sure the witnesses have checked in and he has informed those attending of the evacuation procedure, should there be an air raid. At the opposite side of the room, elevated to the judge's eye level, is the 'dock' accommodating the accused. Prison officers have accompanied Wyeth to court and they sit behind him. On either side of the dock, seats have been put aside for reporters, which have been snapped up very quickly. On the floor, between judge and accused, is a long table reserved for the prosecution, who take two chairs nearest the judge, and the defence, two chairs nearest the accused. Their accumulation of folders and reference documents are piled up on the table before them. Wrottesley glances to his right and offers the briefest of nods toward the 12 men and women of the jury. To his left, more wooden benches accommodate rows of court officials, with one long bench reserved for the witnesses to sit after giving evidence. When they are called, the witnesses must cross in front of the judge, to arrive at the witness stand between judge and jury. Adorned in more wood panelling, the witness stand is not too dissimilar in appearance to a church pulpit. Lastly, set high into the huge vaulted ceiling, beyond the seemingly obligatory wood-panelled balcony, sits the public gallery. It is doubtful any Riddlesworth locals, apart from those called as witnesses, will attend today. Those who are attending include representatives from New Scotland Yard, Captain Stephen Van Neck from

Norfolk County Constabulary and Wyeth's commanding officer from the Pioneer Corps. The judge scans the panorama before him. All seems as it should be, so he makes himself comfortable in his chair.

The clerk of the court rises to begin proceedings. As he stands, the room is hushed to silence. He outlines the charge.

"James Wyeth, you are charged with the murder of Patricia Ann Cupit, on the 6ᵗʰ May last. Are you guilty? Or not guilty?"

Wyeth responds.

"Not guilty."

Those two words will be Wyeth's only contribution to the trial today. For the most part, he will sit void of any emotion, simply staring across the room. He will ask no question, nor will he be called upon. Instead, the trial will focus upon his actions, yet those talking about him will do so as if he is not in the room. The clerk then instructs the jury to swear an oath that they will consider the evidence faithfully in order to reach their verdict. After the swearing in, he tells them:

"Members of the jury, the prisoner at the bar, James Wyeth, is charged with the murder of Patricia Ann Cupit on the 6ᵗʰ May last. To this indictment he had pleaded not guilty, and

it is your charge to say, having heard the evidence, whether he be guilty or not."

The clerk's words simplify the crux of what the jury must consider. He has specifically used the term 'murder', instead of 'kill'. No one, not even the defence team, will argue whether Wyeth's actions snuffed out little Pat's life, yet, does the jury know the distinction between 'killing' and 'murdering'? The latter implies the accused intended the action, which will be the prosecution's argument, backed by many in the public gallery, who believe he should pay for his crime, ultimately with his own life. There will be little sympathy toward any of the defence's arguments suggesting Wyeth was insane when he killed Pat.

Sir Charles Doughty is leading the case for the prosecution. Over the years, he has given counsel at many Old Bailey murder trials, sometimes putting the wrongdoers onto the hangman's gallows. He rises from his chair and outlines his case for the benefit of the judge and jury.

"May it please you, my Lord, members of the jury. You have heard that the accused man, James Wyeth, is charged with the murder of a girl called Patricia Ann Cupit on the 6th May, according to the indictment, because she died on the 6th May. In fact, the act which you will have to enquire into, was committed on Tuesday 5th May.

James Wyeth, as you see, was at that time, and I suppose is today, in the Army, in the Pioneer Corps. The little girl Patricia Ann Cupit, whose body, almost dead, was found on the 5th May in a park known as Riddlesworth Park, which is just in the County of Suffolk, and is almost on the borders of Norfolk and Suffolk. The nearest town to it is Bury St. Edmunds, but it is in a very countrified district.

This little girl was living there with a man and his wife of the name Pask. Mr Pask was a tractor driver engaged in agriculture down there, and this little girl was living there because her parents lived at Norbury and she was evacuated there. She had in fact been evacuated to Norfolk in the previous August. She had been to other places before that, but she was then, and had been since August, living with the Pasks, and was apparently living a perfectly happy and contented life.

At twenty minutes past eight, on the 5th May, or possibly a few minutes before or after, the little girl left the cottage which is known as 'The Stud', or 'The Stud Farm', on the borders of Riddlesworth Park, to go to school. Her course to go to school took her along a pathway right across Riddlesworth Park. Perhaps I had better hand to you now a plan, so that you will see the course which the girl would have to take."

Copies of a map are distributed down the two lines of the jury. The judge is handed his copy. During this time the courtroom is silent, only the sound of maps rustling, as they are passed along and opened up, can be heard. Sir Charles allows time for those receiving them to become accustomed to the layout before he continues. It is vital everyone understands the landmarks of Riddlesworth Park, especially as those landmarks will be frequently referred to over the course of the next two days. He goes on to describe the map, explaining the route Pat would have taken, then moves on to explain what happened on the day Pat was discovered.

"She was not seen during the day, so far as I know, by anybody except the prisoner after she left the Pask's house. She never arrived at the school, and did not get home, as she was expected to do, by about half-past four in the afternoon. At about 5 o'clock, the little girl being then fully half an hour late, even if she had walked slowly and toddled, Mrs Pask became anxious and nervous, and went out into the grounds looking for her. She first of all saw her husband, who had just returned at about the same time, and spoke to him, no doubt, about her anxieties. The husband was in the house, and then there came into the house a boy called Albert Balls. Mr Pask became really alarmed and he and Balls went off to the school to make enquiries as to where this little girl might be.

They found she was not at school, and they found that she had not apparently been there that day. They were returning to the house, and they were going along the path, either with their cycles or on their cycles, I am not sure which, when the boy Balls noticed a hat lying just off the path at a spot on the plan somewhere near the Ladies' Grove, on the lower side of the path and just outside that place called Ladies' Grove. From the hat, which was recognised as the little girl's hat, they looked into the bushes around there, and then they found the child's body, which was in fact covered with coconut matting, except for the feet. The boy Balls and Albert Pask wisely did not interfere with it at all. The child, though not in fact dead, was apparently dead, being covered with this matting. They went towards the school, and there they met one of the school mistresses, in fact the sports mistress, Miss Neal, and Pask spoke to her, and she went and saw the girl lying there, still covered with this coconut matting. She also wisely did not interfere, but at once went back to the school and telephoned for the police and for a doctor.

The doctor arrived a few minutes before the police, and the coconut matting was then removed from off the body of the child. The child was found lying on her back, with her head forced backwards very much, so that her eyes were staring straight up to the sky. Forced back into a depression in the ground which had been made by forcing her head into it. Considerable force must have been used to have made the depression, I will not call it a hole, that would be an exaggeration, but a very considerable depression into which the back of her head had been forced. Upon the left side of the face, and upon the front, there were a number of horrible stabs, deep incised wounds they are called in medical language, obviously made by a sharp instrument. It might have been a bayonet or it might have been a large knife. No instrument has actually been found that can be proved to have caused those injuries. I do not think you need trouble about that. There were a number of deep wounds in the head, all in the neighbourhood of the ear and the throat, which had caused a great deal of bleeding. There were also smaller wounds on the chin, and also around the mouth, and there were bruises as well on the shoulders, and minor injuries of that kind.

The child appeared to be dead, but she was not in fact dead; she was just breathing. The doctor, having found out that she was desperately ill but still alive, had an ambulance sent for. She was taken in the ambulance to the hospital at Bury St. Edmunds, where she was seen by Dr O'Neale, and examined, but she was so ill from shock that nothing could be done for her until the shock was to some extent abated. She was therefore undressed and put to bed, and kept warm, and it was hoped that she might recover sufficiently for more appropriate and perhaps more drastic treatment. However, she did not recover; she died at ten minutes to seven on the morning of Wednesday, 6th May. That she died in consequence of the injuries she had received, there can be no doubt whatever. Whether she bled to death, whether she died from shock, whether she died because her brain was injured through *her head being forced back into the ground, or whether she was partly strangled, because there was evidence of strangulation, does not matter. She died of that multiplication of injuries which had been inflicted upon her.*

Her dress and her petticoat had been pulled up over her body; her drawers or bloomers had been pulled down, exposing all the lower parts – her stomach, her private parts, and her thighs; her drawers were pulled down below her knees, and the legs were spread out about eighteen inches apart. There were marks in the ground as if a man had been kneeling over her, or had probably been in a kneeling position at some time, certainly, and possibly at the time when the injuries were committed. That was the dreadful state of affairs. This poor child who is described as an affectionate, intelligent, healthy, cheerful child, met her death in this way at the hands of someone."

Sir Charles pauses for a moment, offering just enough time for his words to sink in with the jury, but not too long. Too long and he will lose their attention. He scans across them, making eye contact, assessing their reaction while also keeping their attention upon him. It's just a few seconds, the time it takes to inhale a deep lungful of breath before continuing.

Sir Charles now directs the jury to look at the map, upon which the location of the ammunition dump is featured. He highlights the dump as being where Wyeth and his fellow soldiers were sent to work, and it was from there that Wyeth saw Pat walk past. A few seconds later, while he is in mid-flow describing the scene, he is interrupted by Justice Wrottesley.

"The tiny little green square is the dump, is it?"

Sir Charles responds.

"Yes, my Lord."

He turns to look up at Wrottesley, but sees the judge is looking down, focused upon his own map. The judge offers no recognition of Sir Charles' answer. The barrister, presuming the judge has located the dump on the map and needs no further clarification, continues, drawing reference to the map.

"Corporal Molson was in charge of this small party. Private Morgan and Private Woodbridge, and the prisoner, formed this small party. They began work at about a quarter past eight, and you will remember that this little girl passed close to that place along the pathway between twenty minutes past and half past eight. At half past eight the prisoner asked if he might go to the latrines. Permission was granted, and he went off to the latrines, which were up in the wood, some little distance away. You go up that path; that would be the only way to go to the latrines. You probably may come to the conclusion that he did not in fact go to

them. At any rate, he asked for permission to go to the latrines, and permission was granted.

Then Corporal Molson went away to some other job, and came back to the ammunition dump, forty minutes after the prisoner had gone, as he said, to the latrines, and the prisoner had not returned. Corporal Molson then walked up the path towards the latrines, and as he was walking up it, he saw the prisoner coming down towards him. He noticed that the prisoner was flushed and was violently perspiring. That was the 5th May, not a particularly hot day. The Corporal asked him why he was sweating, and the prisoner said, 'It's the weather, don't you think it's hot?'

Members of the jury, he then walked back to his work, and Private Morgan also noticed that he was sweating very heavily, and was red in the face. Private Woodbridge will tell you that he noticed beads of perspiration on the prisoner's face when he returned from this forty minutes' absence. Nothing further happened of any note on that day.

Meanwhile the police were making further enquiries. On the 10th May, a Sunday, the prisoner was seen and asked to make a statement, and that statement will be read to you. It is the first statement he made in which he gave an account of his movements on that day. Members of the jury, he has made a second one entirely contradicting it, but I had better read it to you because it may become of importance at a later stage of this case."

Sir Charles picks up his copy of Wyeth's statement and proceeds to read it out for the benefit of those in the courtroom. Word for word, he takes his time, about three minutes to complete. Once done, he puts the paper statement down, lifts his head to look at the jury again, telling them that Morgan had refuted Wyeth's claim that the two had met when the accused was going to the latrine. Sir Charles suggests this discrepancy is the reason the police asked Wyeth, a few days later, to attend Thetford police station for further questioning, when he then confessed to the attack on Pat. Sir Charles directs the jury to read exhibit 11, which is then handed out to them. This is Wyeth's second statement. Like before, the barrister reads word for word, before emphasising that these are Wyeth's own words. The accused's own admission of the attack.

"This is signed by James Wyeth. That last sentence he wrote himself after having read the statement through. The rest of it was written out by the police at his dictation. That was his own statement of what happened.

His clothes, as I have told you, were taken, and they were sent to Doctor Holden, who will be called before you and who examined the clothes scientifically. He will tell you what he found, but what is more important is that upon Wyeth's blouse there were found three threads which exactly corresponded with a garment which the little girl was wearing. Upon his pullover there was found one thread which exactly corresponded with a thread which also would have come from the clothes which the little girl was wearing on that morning. So that was pretty strong evidence, if you are satisfied that those threads came from the girl's dress, then there had been very close contact between them.

After making that statement, that I have just read to you, the prisoner said he would show the police where this affair took place. He was taken to Riddlesworth Park, and he went over the ground with the police that he had described in that statement, and showed them exactly how he went up the wood and on to the path. Then he walked along the path as he had done when following the girl. He turned off the path and came to the place where the girl's body was found, and he then remarked, which he could not have known, for it was almost impossible for him to have known unless somebody had told him, 'There were more bushes here when I did it'. That was the fact, because the police had, in the course of their enquiries, cut down a number of small gorse and furze bushes when looking for the weapon with which the crime might have been committed. He remembered the place so well that he noticed at once that there had been more bushes about when he committed the crime.

Members of the jury, upon that, he was of course committed for trial, and he now stands upon his trial before you, and if I prove those facts, you will have no doubt at all that this

*man did treat this girl so cruelly that she died. That would be,
and indeed is, murder."*

For Sir Charles, there can be no middle ground, either
Wyeth killed the girl, for which the evidence is
overwhelming, or he didn't. If the jury believe Wyeth did,
then Sir Charles will assert they must find him guilty of
murder. While he has held their focus in his opening
statement, he plants a seed of doubt about the validity of
any forthcoming doctor's report into Wyeth's state of
mind.

*"I have gathered that you will be asked to consider the
state of the prisoner's mind at the time. You might remember
that in his statement of the 14th May he says that he remembers
dragging the girl into the bushes, but then he does not
remember what happened. You will have to consider carefully
how far that part of the statement is true, and whether he did
not remember perfectly well, when he said he felt depressed at
how wicked he had been, the horrible crime which he had
committed. If, members of the jury, it were true that in a
moment of aberration, or one of those curious lapses for which
medical men invent different names at different times, he
had something which he knew was wrong, it is possible, it
will be for your consideration, that if he had within two or
three hours told anybody what he had done, the girl's life
might have been saved. She was still alive at six o'clock that
evening, and did not die until seven o'clock the next morning.*

She had been left there under the sacking all day long, from about half-past eight until nearly six o'clock with those deep wounds in her neck from which she was bleeding.

Members of the jury, those are the facts. With the help of my learned junior, Mr Howard, I will call the evidence before you. The prisoner has the advantage of being defended here before you by my learned friends Mr Alpe and Mr Solomon, and you may be sure, members of the jury, that anything and everything that can be said on his behalf will be said to you."

Sir Charles, after finishing his statement, returns to take his seat at the table in front of the judge. Moments later, the first prosecution witness is called. It is not someone who saw the girl's body lying in the bushes, or even a soldier, but instead it is Edwin Graham, surveyor to Norfolk County Council. Mr Graham drew the map of Riddlesworth Park, the one distributed out a few minutes ago. Proceedings momentarily pause while Graham is shown to the witness stand and takes the witness' oath. Sir Charles' colleague, Gerald Howard, questions Mr Graham, but his queries are purely procedural, with the surveyor simply confirming his name, where he lives, his job at the council and the fact he went to Riddlesworth Park to draw the map. The map is handed to him, and he confirms it is an exact copy. Mr Howard points to various key locations on the map and asks Mr Graham to confirm they are in fact a true representation of the layout of Riddlesworth Park. While this first witness can offer nothing to the guilt, or otherwise, of the accused, he does confirm the map is accurate and fit for purpose. After a few minutes, the questions are over and the witness is free to leave court.

THE PASKS GIVE EVIDENCE

The next witness to be brought before the court is Flo Pask. She offers just one-word answers to each of Sir Charles' questions. For his part, the prosecution barrister does not press her for further clarification. That strategy serves them both well. Flo, who is not comfortable appearing in front of so many people, will not need to contemplate her brief answers, nor elaborate on them, while the prosecution can control the narrative. Flo is compliant to go along with this, the sooner she concludes her time in the witness stand, the sooner she can leave this courtroom. Also, for the first time, she is facing the man who attacked Pat.

After several yes and no answers, Flo has merely confirmed Pat stayed with her, and the girl had left for school after having breakfast. Sir Charles then enquires about what Flo did after realising Pat was missing. It offers nothing new to those following the case.

"Did you get anxious?"

"Yes."

"Did you speak to your husband?"

"Yes."

"Did you go to look for her?"

"Yes."

Sir Charles makes reference to the clothing Pat was wearing when she left home that morning. He pauses, looks toward a court official, then beckons him to hand a piece of evidence to Flo. In the court documents it is listed as exhibit number three. It is Pat's hat. For Sir Charles, detached as he is from the girl, it is merely evidence in his latest case. For Flo, the last time she saw the hat was when Pat was lying lifeless under a tree.

"Is that the little girl's hat?" Sir Charles enquires of Flo.

She hesitates briefly before answering.

"Yes."

Sir Charles then instructs the court official to show her evidence number four.

"Hold the coat up."

Then to Flo he asks:

"Was that the coat which she was wearing?"

"Yes, that is her coat."

She answers in the present tense, as though little Pat might walk through the courtroom at any time to claim her coat back.

Sir Charles presses on with his questions, all matter of fact, asking Flo about the state of Pat's clothing, underwear and the position of the girl's legs when found lying on the ground. Flo's one-word answers at least limit her thoughts going back to relive those gory details while she is stood in the public glare. It is Sir Charles who tells the jury of Pat's injuries, while Flo simply answers yes or no, before he quickly moves on to the next question. After a few minutes of Sir Charles' probing, she is excused from the witness stand and her ordeal is over. The next witness to be called is her husband, Albert Pask.

Neither Albert, or his wife, find this setting comfortable, but for him it cannot be any further from his day-to-day routine. Right now, he would rather be in a Suffolk field, under wide horizons, toiling over the earth with his tractor. While working at the farm, he may go many hours without seeing another soul, hours without conversation, which suits him just fine. It is a stark contrast to the claustrophobic wooden clad interior of this courtroom, where he feels everyone's eyes upon him. Albert appears more nervous than his wife. Maybe it's the nerves, maybe it's the summer heat, but he is sweating under his Sunday best. His mouth is dry. Through his chest, his heart is beating at ten to the dozen. He takes to the stand.

Sir Charles' colleague, Gerald Howard, asks a similar range of questions to those the senior barrister put to Flo Pask. Albert clears his throat and confirms his name, address, job and the fact he is married to the previous witness. He doesn't have to think too hard for those replies, offering him an easy transition toward tougher questions about what happened on the day Pat went missing. Indeed, when Mr Howard enquires if Mrs Pask said anything to him upon realising Pat was not home, the prosecution barrister finishes his sentence with:

"Do not tell us what she said."

Albert's only option is to answer "Yes". Mr Howard also structures his questions in such a manner that Albert can only answer yes or no. Despite this, Albert's nerves rise to the surface. If the prosecution has briefed him about what to say, then, when discussing the location of Pat's hat, he strays from the script.

"Do you know a clump of trees in Riddlesworth Park called Ladies' Grove?" enquires Mr Howard.

"Yes."

"*Was it near there?*" The prosecution anticipates Albert's confirmation that the hat was found at Ladies Grove.

"*I do not know about Ladies' Grove.*"

Albert's answer has contradicted his previous one when he confirmed knowledge of the trees. For Mr Howard, it's a deviation from the script. In his mind, he already had the next question lined up, it just required the witness to confirm with one-word that the hat was found at Ladies Grove. For such an experienced barrister, however, this scenario is not new to him. He pauses for the briefest of moments, to change tack and restructure his line of questioning so Mr Pask can give the expected response.

"*Do you know where the path passes out of the gardens of Riddlesworth Hall, on the left as you go back to your cottage, there is a clump of trees?*"

"*Yes.*"

The prosecution barrister asks again, hoping to receive affirmation it was: "*Was it anywhere near those trees?*"

"*The hat, sir?*" Albert questions.

"*Yes.*" Mr Howard replies.

"*Yes sir.*"

Mr Howard's prompting ensures the courtroom

receives the answer he was expecting, albeit with a slight delay. By any stretch of the imagination, it was not a pivotal question in the proceedings, but the prosecution cannot afford too many deviations from their script. Another minute of questioning passes without incident, then the prosecution are done with this witness. Frank Alpe, leading Wyeth's defence, passes over the opportunity to interrogate Albert further, and the relieved farmer is released from the witness stand.

DOCTOR'S TESTIMONIES

Two more witnesses, Albert Balls, the young lad who, along with Mr Pask, discovered Pat, and Beatrice Neale, the school teacher summoned by Mr Pask, appear one by one in front of the court. Like the Pasks, they offer one-word answers to the prosecution's script to outline events on the evening Pat was found. Alpe takes his first opportunity to question a witness, when he asks Neale:

"*Would it be right to describe what you saw as a tragic and terrible sight?*"

Although she confirms it to be so, it is hard to see how his question will benefit his client. Dr Walton, who attended Pat is given more licence to speak. Sir Charles, rather than directing a question at the doctor, requests the doctor describe what he saw when he arrived at the scene. The doctor, who has many years' experience of relaying traumatic scenes to inquests, replies:

"*I found a little girl about six years old lying on her back, north to south, head to the north and feet to the south. Her head had been pressed; the occipital portion of the skull had made a depression in which it was lying in the soft earth. Her body was exposed. Her knickers had been drawn up so that the anterior portion of her genital organs were exposed. I noticed her head. She had three stab wounds, one beneath the chin to the left-hand side, and one to the right and one to the left of the nose.*"

Justice Wrottesley interrupts for clarification of the wounds.

"*One below the chin?*"

The doctor diverts his eyes from Sir Charles, turns his head left so he ensures the judge is looking at him, then illustrates the injury by putting an index finger under his own chin.

"*One here, and one on either side of the face.*"

"*One on either cheek?*"

"*Yes, and then a small wound in the right ear, I think it was. A bit of the right ear was cut off.*"

"*Cutting a piece out of the ear?*"

"*Yes, out of the tragus. Her left eye was swollen and black. She had an internal squint; the left eye squinted inwards.*"

Sir Charles re-joins the discussion with Dr Walton.

"*Do you think that was the result of violence, or was it natural?*"

Prior to the doctor, the witnesses have been guided along a script when giving their answers, but the doctor, seen as an 'expert' witness, appears more comfortable in the courtroom and is given licence to answer as he sees fit. He feels he has yet to finish his answer to the judge, so he deflects Sir Charles' question for now.

"*I will tell you in a minute, sir, if you will allow me. She was semi-conscious, because she objected to our pushing her over; whenever we tried to move her, she said, ah, ah, don't!*"

Justice Wrottesley again desires clarification and asks if Pat indicated she was in pain. The doctor, offers his answer, demonstrating upon himself with his index finger whenever using the word 'that'.

"*Yes. She was sufficiently conscious to know she had pain. She had two marks on her neck just above the breastbone. The left mark appeared to me to be due to a cord pressed against her neck like **that**. That is how it appeared to me. It was three inches long and half an inch wide, and it was the mark of a cord. I do not think it was tied around her neck. I think it was done like **that**, pressed down against her neck like **that**, making a mark about three inches long.*"

"*You think a cord had been pressed onto her neck in front?*" the judge asks.

"*Yes, on the windpipe, and above that was the mark of a forefinger and thumb, as if he had pressed with his fore-finger and thumb. Above this cord mark was a mark made by a forefinger and thumb, as if pressed against the windpipe. Her face was covered with blood, and her hair was matted with blood.*"

In Sir Charles' opening statement to the court, he mentioned Pat might have been saved if Wyeth, realising the error of his ways, had confessed to the attack and led police to where she lay. Sir Charles raises this point with the doctor.

"*Were her injuries such that her life might have been saved if she had been attended to sooner?*"

"*I understand afterwards that the internal squint in the left eye was due to cerebral haemorrhage. Probably, if we had got to her in time, we could have located that haemorrhage and stopped it.*"

Justice Wrottesley, interrupts again to add his own spin on the question. In his mind, the question is about acting upon the injuries that were obvious when Pat was discovered, not upon what the subsequent autopsy revealed.

"*You are asked for your opinion having regard to what you could see. If she had been discovered soon after the injuries had been done to her, you think she might have recovered?*"

"*Something might have been done, yes, sir. I do think so.*"

Sir Charles is now finished with his questioning of the doctor. Wrottesley looks toward the defence and asks Alpe if he has anything to ask of the witness. The defence barrister says he has, he stands, turning to face the witness, then proceeds to fire off rapid questioning, in stark contrast to how the doctor was questioned by the prosecution. Alpe does not give the doctor any time to elaborate or consider the question. The defence barrister wants to test Sir Charles' approach about the fact Pat might have been saved if she had been found earlier.

"*How many kinds of injuries do you say she had?*"

"*She had wounds …*"

"*What kind of wounds?*"

"*She had some stab wounds.*"

"*What other kind of wounds?*"

"*She had a bit of her ear cut off…*"

"*What was that caused by?*"

"*It was probably struck off with a knife like that.*" The doctor again plays out the motion of his ear being sliced by a knife.

"*And evidence of strangulation?*"

"*Yes, of pressure.*"

"*Did you say she had something round her neck then?*"

"*No, only just like that is how it appeared to me.*"

"*The work of a maniac?*"

"*Well, I do not know. He wanted to get rid of what he had done…*"

"*I am not asking you that. The work of a maniac, doctor?*"

"*Oh … well, I should think he was not quite right at this time.*"

"*I cannot hear you.*"

Alpe invites the doctor to repeat his previous statement that the attacker may not have been in full control of his mental attributes. It may carry weight with the jury if the doctor does.

"*I do not know if he was right at the time, but I should think he wanted to get rid of his victim somehow or other, and he thought by leaving her under that tree she would never have been found at all.*"

"*I suppose a maniac might do that?*"

"*Yes. A maniac may.*"

Alpe, having gained the statement he was fishing for, informs the court he has no further questions. Dr Walton is no longer required, so is excused from the court proceedings.

Two more witnesses are also excused. Barbara Samples, the girls' school headmistress, and John Smith, a lad who saw the commotion on Riddlesworth Park, have come to London to give evidence, but before they can take to the witness stand, Justice Wrottesley informs a court official to tell them they can go home. It seems neither the prosecution or defence see any merit in what those two have to say. Perhaps the case has now moved on beyond simply setting the scene.

The next to appear is another doctor, Daniel O'Meara, a surgeon at the hospital in Bury St. Edmunds, where Pat was taken to. Sir Charles enquires about the sensitive subject of whether Pat was abused during the attack.

"You saw her, I think, when she had been undressed and put to bed?"

"Yes."

"In what condition was she?"

"She was very shocked. Her face and head were covered in blood. There were bruises on the chest and neck, and her condition was more or less hopeless from the time I saw her. She was suffering from very severe shock."

"Had she lost blood?"

"Yes. The face and head were covered with dried blood."

"I think you examined her private parts, did you?"

"Yes."

"Did you find any evidence of any sexual interference?"

"None."

"I think your examination was afterwards confirmed by microscopical examination?"

"I did it at the time by taking slides."

Mr Alpe, wanting the witness to repeat to the jury the fact that Pat had not been abused, requests to question the witness, a request approved by Wrottesley.

"You made a special microscopical examination to see whether there had been any attempt at sexual interference of any sort or kind, did you not?"

"Yes."

"And the results were negative?"

"Yes."

"If there had been, it is quite an easy thing to find, is it not?"

"Comparatively easy."

Wrottesley, looking down upon the witness and using his most stern voice, also requests the witness to repeat the claim that Pat was not abused.

"Do not let us have any doubt about this. Your evidence amounts to this, does it not, that she was not interfered with?
"

Dr O'Meara responds:

"Yes. She was not interfered with."

Sir Charles calls Corporal Edward Molson to the witness stand. The corporal supervised Wyeth at the ammunition dump on the fateful day Pat was attacked and it is the witness' statement to the police the prosecution wants to discuss. Molson says the accused disappeared while he should have been working. The witness then confirms the type of clothing the men were wearing at the time. He is also shown exhibit number seven, Wyeth's denim overalls, to which he confirms they look like the accused's. Once the prosecution has finished their questions, Alpe is given his chance to cross-examine the witness, but declines to do so. The defence's case is built on Wyeth's state of mind, so they have no need to highlight the forensic science confirming he was at the scene of the attack, nor witness statements confirming he went missing at the time. Molson is therefore dismissed from the witness stand, but Sir Charles is perturbed by the defence's lack of questioning. He states he plans to call two more soldiers as witnesses, but they will say much the same as Molson. With the defence seemingly not bothered about what they have to say, Sir Charles approaches Justice Wrottesley.

"My Lord, as there has been no cross-examination of Molson, I think it is a waste of time to call Morgan."

The judge acknowledges the suggestion with a slight nod, agrees with Sir Charles and then looks beyond the prosecution to direct a question to the defence barrister.

"*Do you want Morgan, Mr Alpe?*"

"*No, my Lord.*" Alpe responds.

Justice Wrottesley then informs a court official to tell the soldiers – Morgan and Woodbridge; they are not required, meaning they too have been compelled to come to London, only to be sent home before appearing as witnesses.

THE POLICE

The prosecution now turns its attention to calling police witnesses. Police Constable Arthur Youngs and Detective Inspector William Garner, both from Norfolk County Constabulary, relay their recollections of what they saw when they arrived at the scene.

Youngs informs the court he accompanied Pat to hospital and retained her hat for forensics. For his part, Garner confirms he took Wyeth's clothing for forensic testing when the accused came to Thetford police station. Sir Charles questions the latter about this. Garner confirms Wyeth asked to speak with Chief Inspector Barratt and that Wyeth then confessed to attacking Pat. Under Sir Charles' cross-examination, Garner also tells the court that Wyeth even took the police to the scene of the attack.

"Were you also present when the defendant took Mr Barratt and indicated to him a route through the wood and through the park?"

"Yes."

"The next day at about twenty minutes to one, in the morning of the day, did you again caution the defendant?"

"Yes."

"And charge him with the murder of this little girl?"

"Yes, I did."

"Did he say anything?"

"No, he made no reply, sir."

Sir Charles, having highlighted evidence that Wyeth fully remembered attacking Pat and where it happened, concludes his questioning. The judge enquires with the defence if they wish to ask questions, but Mr Alpe tells him he has none, so the detective is allowed to leave.

The next witness is Dr Henry Smith Holden, the police forensics officer who received Wyeth's clothing for testing. The doctor is handed a paper bag with evidence contained inside. It is clothing, the same clothing he tested at the police laboratory. Sir Charles asks the doctor what is inside the bag,

"*Did you receive the pink clothing of the little girl and the denim blouse, trousers, and pullover?*"

The doctor confirms he did and that those are the garments inside the bag he has just been given. Wrottesley interrupts Sir Charles' questions to enquire which item of clothing he will be referring to first. Sir Charles' turns from the witness, looks up to the judge and answers:

"*The trousers, my Lord.*"

Sir Charles then returns to the witness for his questions.

"*Look at the trousers. Are there on the left and right legs of those denim trousers any blood marks?*"

"*There are, of human blood.*"

"*I think there is also a splash on the edge of the pocket on the left-hand side?*"

"*Yes.*"

"*And slight smears on the lining of the left pocket on the front of the left leg?*"

"*Yes.*"

"*Of human blood?*"

"*Of human blood,*" the doctor confirms.

The two men then discuss the fibres found on Wyeth's clothing, matching those from Pat's. Surprisingly Frank Alpe does not ask any questions. He might have tested the forensics and how they had matched the human blood on Wyeth's clothing to that of Pat. He might have asked if the blood was Wyeth's own, or indeed anyone else's. Had the blood got there through some accident at work? How did the forensics officer conclude it was specifically Pat's? There may be questions about the procedure preventing Wyeth's clothing being contaminated by the fibres from Pat's clothing when they were packed for testing. Alpe could have even taken the prosecution to task over the murder weapon not having been found. He doesn't. Instead, he tells Justice Wrottesley he has no questions. Perhaps the question that needed asking most, is the fact the murder weapon has never been found.

It has been a long day of questioning. The clerk of the court draws today's hearing to a close, telling the courtroom it is now adjourned until 11am tomorrow morning. The prosecution, having taken the lead, have been happy to use today to replay events around the killing and Wyeth's admission. There has been little opportunity for the defence to prove Wyeth's mental state played a part, but they will get their chance tomorrow, when they hope to bring the weight of medical science and psychology to the witness stand. They will also put Wyeth's mother in the spotlight, in what promises to be an emotional testimony.

CHIEF INSPECTOR BARRATT GIVES EVIDENCE
FRIDAY, 17TH JULY, 1942

Sunderland Daily Echo – *Defence submission of insanity. Three small threads have been produced as evidence at the Old Bailey.*

Birmingham Mail – *Evacuee's death. The prosecution allege that the threads were taken from Wyeth's battledress and that they are similar to threads from the girl's clothing.*

The Shields Evening News – *Threads as evidence in murder trial. Wyeth is alleged to have made a statement that he followed the girl to a clump of trees, where he got her by the neck and dragged her away.*

Liverpool Daily Post – *Soldier on murder charge. James Wyeth, aged 22, of Cedar Road, Maidenhead, a private in the Pioneer Corps, pleaded not guilty.*

Back in May, when the story broke about Pat being attacked, the newspapers were awash with graphic reports of what happened. Most of those were syndicated, with newspaper editions across Britain printing the same report, apart from the Daily Mirror which had exclusive access to Pat's parents. But, when the police made little progress, the interest of the newspaper editors waned. Then, with Wyeth's arrest, and his subsequent appearance at the East Harling hearing, the newspapers saw another surge of column inches given to the tragedy. Since then, the story has disappeared totally, the editors having more pressing stories to follow up. The war is not going well. In North Africa the Germans have taken Tobruk, leading to the surrender of tens of thousands of Allied servicemen. In the Atlantic Ocean, German U-boats are sinking Allied convoys at will, while in the Pacific, the Americans offered a glimmer of hope when they inflicted a heavy defeat on the Imperial Japanese Navy, in the Battle of Midway. Yet, yesterday's court hearing saw Wyeth hit the headlines once again with a fervour not seen since his arrest. All reports focus on his alleged guilt. There is no doubt the reporters have an appetite for today's hearing, when they expect Wyeth to be found guilty. They also expect Wrottesley to administer the 'coup de grace' when he sentences the accused to death. There is little sympathy for Pat's attacker. Many consider the world to be a better place without him, and it is predicted the newsstands will alert the nation to how the trial ended. The conclusion of the trial will therefore signal the beginning of the race to see which edition will be first to get their report circulated. Some may even make publication in time to be sold this evening. Not just in London, but across the nation, the anticipated hanging of a child killer could be just the antidote to wipe the bad news from the front pages.

Inside the courtroom, the clerk brings the room to a hush. Although the prosecution was allocated time yesterday to outline their case, they also begin the second day's proceedings. They call Chief Inspector Thomas Barrett to the witness stand. Barratt has conducted his investigation with impartiality, focusing on the evidence and without speculation of the motive or the accused's state of mind. This may well be tested now. Sir Charles questions Barrett about when the detective met Wyeth for the first time. He wishes to examine Wyeth's statement about what he was doing on the morning Pat was attacked. Unlike the other expert witnesses, Barratt does not elaborate, but instead simply confirms or denies the questions put to him. Again, demonstrating he is here purely for the facts as he saw them and to offer them impartially.

"*On that occasion was he cautioned?*" Sir Charles asks.

"*No, sir,*" Barratt replies.

"*You had no reason at that time for contemplating arresting him?*"

"*No, sir.*"

"*I think he made a statement, which Sergeant Webb wrote down?*"

"*Yes.*"

"*Was it then read over to him?*"

"*Yes, sir.*"

"*Did he sign it?*"

"Yes."

The actual statement is handed to Barratt. He takes a look and confirms it is the one Wyeth signed. Before Sir Charles can continue, Wrottesley interrupts, requesting to see the document. The judge is very thorough and if evidence is going to be presented in court, then he demands to see it. A court official steps over, collects it from Barratt, and a few steps later ensures the judge is in possession of Wyeth's statement. The judge looks down toward it, then looks up to Barratt and turns the document to face the detective.

"Is this the document?" he asks.

"Yes, my Lord," Barratt replies.

The judge then requests the statement be read out to the whole court, despite Sir Charles already reading it out, word for word, in his opening statement yesterday. Sir Charles again addresses the jury:

"Members of the Jury, I have read this statement to you before, and I think it is better, now that it is being formally proved, that it should be read again. This is the statement of James Wyeth, Private, Number 13089701, 218 Company, Pioneer Corps."

Sir Charles spends a few minutes reading through his own copy, while Wrottesley follows, word for word, on the actual statement handed to him. When Sir Charles concludes his reading, the judge confirms his approval by simply saying:

"*Yes, that is right.*"

Sir Charles, having navigated the disruption, continues his questioning of Barratt, requesting the detective go over the events of the morning of Wyeth's arrest. The barrister is experienced enough to know the golden rule when questioning witnesses - he must not present a leading question, one that contains the answer in the question. However, this rule has seemingly been up for loose interpretation, and leading questions have been allowed so far. Sir Charles asks Barratt:

"*I think when you got to the Thetford Police Station you said to him, did you not? 'You know who I am?'*"

Although Barratt confirms it to be the case, Wrottesley intervenes and asks Sir Charles:

"*There is no objection, I presume, to your leading there?*"

Sir Charles is momentarily taken aback. He turns toward Frank Alpe, looking for a response, but the barrister offers the merest shake of the head to indicate no objection. Sir Charles responds to Wrottesley's question:

"*No, I have been informed so, my Lord.*"

Sir Charles, having satisfied the judge's concern,

returns to questioning Barratt, although putting more words in the mouth of the detective, none of which are objected to by the defence.

"*I think you then said, I have made enquiries into the statement you made on Sunday as to your movements on the 5ᵗʰ May? 'I am not satisfied with your explanation. Is there anything else you can tell me, or any person that I can see to enable me to satisfy myself that what you have told me is true?' What was his reply to that?*"

"*He said, I've told you the truth.*"

"*Then you told him that other clothing would be obtained for him, and that you wanted possession of what he was wearing for examination?*"

"*Yes, sir.*"

"*I think at 11 o'clock, before the fresh clothing arrived, he again spoke to you and said this, did he not? 'I remember now, sir, that I took off my denim blouse when I went to the lavatory that morning, and on my way back from the lavatory I dropped it in on my bunk in the hut. I saw Private Montague, the Billet Orderly, either at break or at dinner that day, and he told me he had found my blouse and put it in my valise for me.*'"

"*Yes.*"

Rather than asking Barratt what happened – the

detective is an expert witness, after all, one who compiled a report on the investigation into Pat's attack – Sir Charles appears to merely seek approval of his own narrative. The jury members are hearing more from Sir Charles, less from the man who apprehended Pat's attacker. Sir Charles goes on to question Barratt about Wyeth's second statement, the one given at Thetford police station, where Wyeth admitted to the attack. Sir Charles asks a court official for Wyeth's second statement, again Wrottesley requests the original is handed to him so he can personally confirm it to be true while Sir Charles reads a copy. The judge then turns to Barratt, and asks if the statement was written by the detective. Barratt declares it was, apart from the last sentence, which Wyeth added in his own handwriting. Sir Charles turns to Barratt, again seeking approval of his own narrative.

"*After the statement had been taken, did he then say to you, 'I can't remember anything else, sir, but I can take you and show you where I went?'*"

"*Yes.*"

"*I think you again cautioned him and said, 'Do you want to do that?' He said, 'Yes, sir.' Then he went, I think with Sergeant Webb, Inspector Garner, and yourself to Riddlesworth Camp?*"

"Yes, sir."

"Did he then take you and show you the ammunition dump which is marked on the plan produced?"

"Yes."

"I think, Inspector, you had better now follow this with the plan."

Barratt is handed the map. Sir Charles instructs him to hold it up, so it faces the jury. The detective is then asked to point to the map to show the location of the ammunition dump. The map is very large and has been folded whilst in storage. Just below a fold in the paper, Barratt sees a turquoise mark indicating Mr Tortice's home. Just above that, Barratt puts his index finger on the map. Sir Charles then asks him to trace the journey Wyeth took, from the dump, through the woods and along a path toward where Pat was attacked. While Barratt speaks, Wrottesley, looking at his own copy of the map, becomes lost and asks Sir Charles for clarification on the path Wyeth took.

"I have in my copy, a hut which is marked "N.A.A.F.I."

Sir Charles responds, *"It is not that path, my Lord. It is the next path."*

Sir Charles pauses, his frown betraying the fact he is now lost too. He then backtracks to confirm the path is the one the judge enquired about.

"I beg your pardon, my Lord. The path that he took was the path running past the hut which is marked N.A.A.F.I."

Justice Wrottesley is still lost, so he and Sir Charles spend a few moments backtracking over the map to clarify what is going on. The judge, upon finding Barratt's position on the map, does not indicate proceedings can continue, instead Sir Charles pauses just long enough until the lack of another question from the judge infers consent to continue. The short-lived silence is broken by Sir Charles, who returns to Barratt, asking about Wyeth's movements. Barely thirty seconds pass before Wrottesley again stops Barratt in mid-sentence. The judge is adamant to not let any small detail pass him by, especially concerning the layout of the map in reference to the scene of the attack. He repeatedly asks Barratt for clarification on certain points, often interjecting Sir Charles' examination. Every time the detective supplies an answer, the judge comes back with another question.

"In my copy, 'woodland path' appears written above the path. Not below?"

"Yes, my Lord."

"He crossed below the lower (telegraph) pole?"

"Yes, my Lord."

"It goes down the footpath below?"

"Yes, my Lord. That is a ditch at the side of the path, there coming from the field, and the part marked in yellow is the footpath."

"A military pathway?"

"Yes, my Lord."

"Where did he join that path?"

"From the corner of that path where the angle comes."

"At the corner of the one with the two poles?"

"Yes, my Lord."

The judge is keenly demonstrating he must be in full possession of the facts, and for him Wyeth's movements on the map are crucial to this case. It will show that Wyeth stalked the girl along Riddlesworth Park, then attacked her in such a savage manner that she later died. However, no one denies this to be true, in fact it is accepted by the defence too. Therefore, are Wyeth's movements really that crucial? The defence might see this exchange as trivial and taking up their valuable time later. They might even consider an objection to the questioning. They, however, don't object. Can anyone really object to the judge's questions? The defence team sit, watching this play out, allowing Sir Charles to resume his questions once the judge stops his. Barratt goes on to explain how Wyeth led the police to the spot where Pat was attacked and the route he took in returning to the ammunition dump. Again, Wrottesley interrupts for clarification on the map. The judge asks Barratt to hold the map up again, for the benefit of the jury, and trace Wyeth's movements on it. Every time Barratt explains a location along the route, the judge insists on clarification. Finally, after Barratt concludes his account, the questions about the map cease. Sir Charles then declares to the courtroom he has finished his questioning of Barratt.

Justice Wrottesley turns to the defence barrister and asks if he has any questions. Frank Alpe was relatively quiet yesterday, allowing the prosecution to outline their case, but today is his day. He tells the judge he does indeed have questions. However, he is not interested in what happened on the day Pat was attacked, it seems the prosecution have already covered enough of that, but the defence barrister wants to know if Chief Inspector Barratt had discovered anything about Wyeth's state of mind. This is Alpe's strategy for today, not whether Wyeth carried out the attack, but instead that Wyeth was insane when he did so. The barrister stands from his chair, looks at Barratt and opens his questioning. He wants to know about Wyeth's natural mother.

"*I do not know whether you can help me, Chief Inspector.*

I want to ask you a few questions about his mother."

"Yes."

"Do you know if his mother at a quite early age was in an institution? Can you help me about that?"

"At the time when the prisoner was born, or just prior?"

"No, before then. Perhaps you cannot help me."

"She was put into a Home."

"A Certified Industrial School at Bath?"

"In a Home at Bath at the age of thirteen, as she had been left without a mother."

"I have got a Certified Industrial School. Afterwards she was a woman who tramped the country, was she not?"

"Yes."

"Selling various things at doors and getting a living how she could?"

"Yes, that is correct."

"Living rough. She was a gypsy woman, was she not?"

"She associates with gypsies now, and has done."

"When the accused was born, I think she did not provide for him; in fact, she was prosecuted for neglect?"

"That is so."

"And the police and the Society for the Protection of Cruelty to Children took the case up and got him adopted by Mrs Wyeth?"

"That is correct."

"Has this woman a daughter?"

"Olive Kathleen Crane, sir."

"Do you know where she is?"

"She is in a public institution at Haverfordwest."

"Is she epileptic?"

"Yes."

"I want to ask you something about the mother's sister, Alice Crane. Was she at one time in the Brampton State Institution for Mental Defectives?"

"Yes."

"With dangerous and violent propensities?"

Wrottesley intervenes, *"She was in a Home for mental defectives, was she?"*

"Yes, my Lord", replies Barratt.

"Where?"

"Brampton State Institution, Northampton."

Alpe probes further about the institutionalisation of Wyeth's family. He has already gained an insight into it from Barratt, which has played into his gameplan. The terminology used in 1940s Britain may not seem appropriate in modern day Britain.

"*Is that a Home for mental defectives of dangerous and violent propensities?*"

"*I do not know about dangerous and violent. It is a Home for feeble-minded persons and mental defectives.*"

Wrottesley again interjects and questions Frank Alpe.

"*Does it say any particular class of mental defectives?*"

"*No, my Lord, my particulars are … a Home for feeble-minded and mentally defective children.*"

Alpe, assuming the judge is satisfied with the answer, returns to question Barratt.

"*Is she at present in the Moss Side State Institution?*"

"*Yes*"

Wrottesley is not yet finished and interrupts Alpe's questioning.

"*Still as a mental defective?*"

"*As a feeble-minded person she is there, my Lord,*" replies Barratt.

Once again, Alpe pauses for the judge, but no further questions come, so the barrister continues his questioning of Barratt.

"Did you make any enquiries of the Board of Control?"

"No, sir, I did not. Enquiries were made at the Institution."

"Look at that," Alpe tells Barratt.

Alpe now goes on the offensive. He has contacted the institution where Wyeth's aunt is a patient and has obtained a document from there. He holds it up, directing it toward Barratt. The document is passed to a court official, who in turn steps across the courtroom to hand it to Barratt. The barrister continues:

"It does say on that letter from the Board of Control …"

Wrottesley interrupts Alpe in mid-flow and asks him if he is submitting the letter as evidence. The barrister replies he is. Wrottesley then, while sternly looking down at Alpe, informs the court that, as the judge presiding over the case, he must look at the letter himself before anyone else. The court official now diverts from Barratt and heads toward the judge. The judge is handed the document and considers the letterhead before responding to Alpe.

"It is from the Board of Control."

"Yes, my Lord," replies Alpe.

"I think I had better read this. Do you want it read?"

"Yes, if your Lordship would."

Wrottesley proceeds to read it aloud for the benefit of those in the courtroom. Once concluded, he puts the letter down, looks toward Alpe and questions the validity of the document as evidence.

"It would appear that in 1926-27 it was NOT an institution for mental defectives of dangerous and violent propensities. It does not say anything here about the Moss Side Institution."

Nonetheless, in anticipation the defence will likely refer to it at some later point, the judge instructs a court official to list the letter as 'exhibit number fourteen'. He goes on to ask Alpe if there are any more questions, but the barrister replies he is now finished. Wrottesley then looks over to the prosecution and asks if they have any, to which Sir Charles suggests he would like to ask a couple more before they let Barratt go. What those questions provide in connection with Wyeth's guilt is debatable.

"You said that his mother had associated with gypsies latterly?"

"Yes."

"As far as you know, is she of gypsy breeding?"

"No. She was one of a family of nine children living under normal circumstances, with nothing to indicate that she was

of gypsy birth, but she has practically the whole of her life associated with gypsies travelling the country."

Barratt is then dismissed from the witness stand, but Sir Charles is far from done. Yet more prosecution witnesses are called. Next up is James Webster, the police forensics officer. Webster is questioned about the various injuries Pat suffered. In an earlier statement, Sir Charles suggested that Wyeth could have saved Pat's life if he had alerted the police to what he had done, rather than leave her body under a tree. Sir Charles wants to emphasise that fact. He asks Webster if Pat would have been saved if found earlier, but is taken aback when Webster answers:

"No, sir."

"Do you not think so?" Sir Charles repeats his question, but Webster is not changing his mind.

"I do not think so. Her injuries, except for certain incised wounds, had not been caused by any other instrument except the hands. She had the following wounds upon her …"

Wrottesley interrupts to prompt the same question at the witness, perhaps testing the expert's testimony.

"In your view, nothing would have saved her life?"

"No, my Lord."

"She had suffered such injuries that treatment would not have saved her?"

"No, my Lord."

"Even if her body had been found earlier?"

"No, my Lord."

With Webster so adamant he has given an honest appraisal, the prosecution and judge drop their line of questioning. Sir Charles now turns his attention to the gruesome nature of the wounds inflicted upon Pat. Keen to highlight the simple truth that Wyeth attacked Pat in such a brutal manner that she had no chance of surviving her wounds, Sir Charles repeatedly asks questions about those injuries, and Wyeth's contribution to them. Webster's responses, describing the wounds, rams home in the jury's mind the involvement of Wyeth in Pat's death. Sir Charles also explores the possibility of Pat having been sexually abused during the attack, but Webster's last statement is to confirm that this was not the case. Frank Alpe, not wanting to give any more air time to discussion of Pat's injuries, declines an offer to ask questions of Webster and the witness is dismissed.

The prosecution has just one more witness, the police photographer who took images of Riddlesworth Park and of the injuries inflicted upon Pat. These photographs are handed to Wrottesley. The defence and the jury have copies too. The images of poor Pat, lying naked on the coroner's table, make for grim viewing, but for the prosecution they are timely, following on from the previous witness' description of them. The prosecution's final act, by distributing these photographs, is to remind the jury that whatever the defence goes on to say, this trial is all about an innocent little girl who had her life cruelly taken away by a man who viciously attacked her. As the prosecution has demonstrated, James Wyeth was that man. After the witness has left, Sir Charles addresses Wrottesley.

"My Lord. I will read the statement of the accused."

Sir Charles, then reads aloud Wyeth's statement, the one when the accused admitted to the attack on Pat. In doing so, Sir Charles makes the distinct connection between the images of a poor girl lying dead on the coroner's table, with Wyeth admitting to causing her horrendous injuries. Sir Charles then concludes the prosecution case.

"He said, not guilty, and he reserved his defence. That, my Lord, is the case for the prosecution."

THE DEFENCE OF WYETH

Finally, into the afternoon of the second day of a two-day trial, the floor is handed over to the defence. Frank Alpe, leading the defence, is the son of a chemist from Wymondham, in Norfolk, just twenty miles from Thetford. Before entering into law, he inherited his father's chemist shop, where he worked as a chemist, and locally featured in amateur dramatics performances. Home is still in Wymondham, where he volunteers as an air raid warden, and his house is a relatively large one, with a tennis court, that he shares his wife, Hilda. As an experienced barrister he spends most of his time in London, staying at his 'work home', in Temple, London, near to the courts and saving him the hours of train commute from Norfolk. He stands before the courtroom, his opening statement shorter than that of Sir Charles'.

"May it please you, my Lord. Members of the Jury. You may have realised by now that it is not strongly contested, if at all, that this man attacked this little girl at Riddlesworth Park on that May morning and inflicted these terrible wounds, and it may be the question you have to determine is – was he in the legal sense sane, or insane, when he did it? The verdict I am going to ask you to return after you have heard my evidence is – guilty, but insane.

Until this affair took place, this young man, apparently,

according to his adopted mother, did not know that he was not her own son. In 1921 an advertisement appeared in the South Wales Echo asking someone to give a home to a baby, and Mrs Wyeth, who adopted him, answered the advertisement. She had lost her child, and she wanted to adopt one. An Inspector of the Society for the Prevention of Cruelty to Children called on Mrs Wyeth, and she adopted the accused man. She will be able to tell you, members of the jury, something about his early history and his history up to the time when he joined the Army, and you may well come to the conclusion, if you accept her evidence, that this accused man has always been abnormal. She will tell you that as a young child he screamed terribly at the sight of a man; she will tell you how on a farm, for some unknown reason, he was riding a horse about and he rode it at some little girl and injured her, she will tell you that on some other occasion he pushed a little girl into a gate and injured her, and other things he did. She will tell you he was brought before the Justices for those offences, and some authority or other sent him to Hereford Hospital, where, as she will tell you, he was examined by a mental specialist, or a doctor who specialises in mental diseases, and he was detained there.

You may well come to the conclusion, the onus is, of course, upon me and my learned friend to satisfy you, that at the time this man did this horrible and dreadful deed he was insane or his mind was affected. Of course, you will take the law in this case, as in every other case, from my Lord, and I speak subject to correction of anything I say to you, but the way I desire you to judge this case after you have heard all the evidence, members of the jury, heard my learned friend Sir Charles Doughty, and heard his Lordship sum, is this. If you could detach yourselves from this Court and consider, when you are carrying out your own business in your own everyday walk of life, that you had heard this evidence then for the first time, I suggest to you, members of the jury, that you would come to one conclusion only, that a man with abnormalities such as I am going to bring evidence before you to prove, the man who committed this dreadful, horrible deed on this little girl, must have been abnormal; his mind must have been affected. I am calling before you, members of the jury, a doctor who specialises in mental disease, and he will tell you his opinion that this man did not know what he was doing; at the time he did not know he was doing wrong.

I will now call my evidence before you."

EVELYN WYETH'S EVIDENCE

Frank Alpe calls his first witness. By entering the witness box, the woman demonstrates an unwavering love for James Wyeth, despite him being so vilified by the newspapers and general public. She has been the only person in his life to have stood by him, through thick and thin, and she is not going to desert him now. She is Evelyn Wyeth, here to save her 'Jim'.

She takes to the witness stand, glances over to her son and offers him a smile. A friendly face among strangers talking about him. He returns no emotion to her. Alpe knows he needs to bring emotion to the proceedings before he introduces his facts. In Evelyn, he has a solid witness, she having sat through court hearings before, so is less daunted by her surroundings than some witnesses called by the prosecution early yesterday. The barrister asks Evelyn about when she adopted Wyeth and his subsequent development as a child.

"*Did you see an appeal in the South Wales Echo in 1921?*"

"*Yes, sir.*"

"*Tell the jury what that was about.*"

"*It was an appeal for someone to give a helpless baby a home, and I answered it.*"

"*I think you had lost your child, had you not?*"

Evelyn briefly hesitates before answering. Her eyes look down toward the floor, then, holding her head back up, she returns to look Alpe in the eye and respond.

"*Yes.*"

Alpe, for his part, does not dwell on the question and quickly presses on.

"*Had there been some trouble in the police court about this mother?*"

"*Yes, she had abandoned him.*"

"*Did you adopt him?*"

"*Yes, sir.*"

"*What did you find about him soon after you had adopted him when he was a baby? Did he cry?*"

"*Well, he was simply terrified of us all. He never cried out loud enough. I never heard him cry out loud.*"

"*How did he cry?*"

"*Silently, always.*"

"*How old was he when he did that?*"

"*Fifteen months.*"

Frank Alpe continues his quick-fire questions, with Evelyn painting a picture of her 'Jim' as being a very troubled child who screamed for long periods, with the child often becoming hysterical. It was a year before Wyeth got used to Evelyn's husband and didn't scream whenever he saw him. Alpe enquires about the age her son began walking. Evelyn confirms he was three years old, which draws astonishment from Justice Wrottesley. The judge enquires of Evelyn if that is true. She confirms the statement is correct. The barrister now wants Evelyn to talk about another episode her son had when he was young.

"Do you remember when he was about four and a half? Anything about sunstroke?"

"Yes, he had a very bad temperature for two days. Screaming."

"Did you have to take him to the doctor?"

"I had to fetch the doctor."

"What did the doctor diagnose?"

"Sunstroke."

"What did he do when he saw the doctor?"

"He was more or less in a high temperature and screaming, and took no notice of the doctor any more than he did of anyone else. He was just screaming the whole of the time because he could see animals coming off the wall."

Alpe, keen to emphasise how this episode affected Wyeth's mental health, repeats Evelyn's last sentence, yet turns it into a question to her. This tactic is for the benefit of the jury, one to highlight the fact that Wyeth was never 'normal' as a child.

"He could see animals coming off the wall?"

"Yes."

"That was what he said, was it?"

"*Yes, sir.*"

"*When he was four and a half, would he talk to other children?*"

"*He had only just started to talk at about four.*"

"*When he started to talk, would he talk to other children or to anyone else?*"

"*No, sir.*"

Again, Wrottesley asks Evelyn to confirm her statement about Wyeth's late development.

"*He talked at four, but not to other children. Is that right?*"

"*Yes, my Lord,*" she answers.

Alpe resumes his questions, again enquiring about Wyeth's slow development, especially as a sociable child.

"*Did he play with other children?*"

"*No, sir.*"

"*Never played with other children?*"

"*No, sir.*"

"*Did he remain like that for several years?*"

"*He has always been like it, sir.*"

Having discussed Wyeth's unsociable attitude, Alpe then questions Evelyn about her son being detained after appearing before local magistrates. It is the elephant in the room for the defence, Wyeth has his criminal past, yet the defence will not want to dwell on it. Through all this, Alpe never mentions Wyeth by name, nor refers to him as being Evelyn's son, only by the terms 'he', 'him' or 'the accused'. The defence barrister asks Evelyn to describe the injuries Wyeth inflicted upon young girls over the years, which usually amounted to cuts and bruises. Having outlined Wyeth's troubled past, Alpe then turns his focus to the medical care given while Wyeth was held on remand.

"*Do you remember him going to Hereford Remand Home?*"

"*Yes.*"

"*Were you directed to take him to the Hereford Hospital?*"

"*Yes, sir.*"

"*By whom was that?*"

"*By the court. I had to fetch him every Saturday morning from the remand home and take him to a mental doctor at the Hereford Hospital.*"

"*That was what the court ordered, was it?*"

"*Yes, sir, the court ordered me to take him to the hospital at Hereford.*"

This latest exchange provides the first formal reference in this trial to Wyeth having received an examination for mental health. This is exactly the route Alpe needs to explore. Wrottesley is also interested and asks Evelyn:

"To see a doctor?"

"Yes, every Saturday morning," she replies.

Alpe continues, employing his tactic of using his witness' answer as a question, so it is repeated in the courtroom.

"What sort of doctor was it, you say?"

"A man that was for the brain. I really could not tell you his name."

"A man for the brain, you said, did you not?"

"Yes, a mental doctor."

Alpe now explores the brutal attack on the young female cyclist. Wyeth's actions in that attack are expanded upon, with Alpe asking Evelyn if she can recall the "incident". She does, and answers in full.

"He came to me one morning after a 12-hours shift, and I asked him to wash and get to bed. He looked very ill and tired. He was a pieceworker. He said he wanted cigarettes first, so I asked him to take the money and bring me some, because I wanted a smoke. He went out, and he did not return that day. At seven in the evening a car drew up, and a police officer got out and told me he had been locked up."

"*What was that for?*" Alpe enquires.

"*He was sitting on a bank smoking a cigarette, with his bicycle lying by his side. A young lady rode by, got off, rode back past him, and he got up and pulled her off her bike, and dragged her about on the floor, treating her very roughly.*"

"*He attacked her, you mean?*"

"*Yes.*"

"*Was he brought before the police court for that?*"

"*Yes, sir.*"

"*What did they say about him?*"

"*They detained him for a week, sir.*"

"*What did they say about him?*"

"*They told me they had a test of his blood, and he had a kink.*"

Is Evelyn implying a blood test on Wyeth concluded he had mental illness? The judge wants to explore this further and make sure her account is correct. He asks her if she actually attended the court hearing following the attack on the cyclist, to which she confirms she had.

"*Yes, sir. I have been to every court.*"

"*You were there?*"

"*Yes.*"

"*What did they say?*"

Evelyn then repeats her claim about the blood test, but this is not backed up by any evidence. Wrottesley enquires if Alpe will call a doctor as a witness to endorse Evelyn's claim. Alpe says he does indeed have a doctor, but they know nothing about the blood test. The judge orders Evelyn's comment to be struck from the record and not considered as part of the proceedings. The judge then takes up the questioning of Evelyn about what happened to Wyeth after the attack. He asks her what punishment Wyeth received.

"*He was sent out on bail for six weeks, and brought up at Kingston Quarter Sessions, and there he was sent away for three years.*" Evelyn replies.

"*Sent to borstal for three years?*"

"*Yes, and the doctor there told me he was being detained.*"

"*The doctor told you?*"

"*Yes.*"

Sir Charles stands up and requests permission to question the witness. This is given.

"*The doctor at borstal?*" he asks Evelyn.

"*The borstal doctor, sir,*" she replies.

Wrottesley is once again concerned about Evelyn's

unsubstantiated claims. He enquires if the borstal doctor Evelyn is referring to is one of Alpe's witnesses. It appears the longer Evelyn speaks, the more her testimony is brought into question. Alpe is unable to corroborate what she is saying, so his response has a rather apologetic tone.

"*We have written for a report from the doctor, but we have not received it up to the present moment.*"

No sooner has Alpe finished his sentence, when Sir Charles steps in with a response to the judge. He knows the borstal medical officer, Dr Grierson, has compiled a report, but due to the doctor's busy schedule the doctor has been unable to attend court today.

"*My Lord, I do not want to intervene, but Dr Grierson at present has a report from the doctor at borstal.*"

Wrottesley suggests getting the report brought to court as soon as possible. He also suggests it is time to move away from this line of questioning to Evelyn. At least until access is gained to the doctor, or his report. Alpe informs the judge he is finished with asking his witness questions, so now it is Sir Charles who faces Evelyn. The prosecution's questions will be less sympathetic to Wyeth's upbringing. In fact, they will aim to show how normal the accused's upbringing was.

"*Mrs Wyeth, at school, this boy got on quite all right, did he not?*"

"*He was never brilliant, sir.*"

"*I did not say he was brilliant, but he got on all right?*"

"*Always a good character.*"

"*And he got on quite well with his teacher and with the other school children?*"

"*Yes, sir.*"

"*Since he left school, he has always earned his living, has he not?*"

"*Yes, sir.*"

"*There was this trouble at Hereford with a little girl, we know, and in consequence of that, after a short time at an Approved School, he went to the 'Cornwall' Training Ship, did he not?*"

"*Yes.*"

"*That did him an immense amount of good, did it not?*"

"*Yes, sir.*"

"*He was a small, bright, intelligent boy when he came back from there, was he not?*"

"*Well, I have never known him really intelligent, sir, because I could never understand him.*"

"*He was eighteen, and he got a job first of all at the Tesco Stores in Maidenhead, where you were then living?*"

"*Yes, sir.*"

"*Then he got a better job at the Western Biscuit Company in Slough?*"

"*Yes.*"

"*And he got the responsible position of an assembler, did he not?*"

"*Yes, sir, but may I explain how he got those jobs? I got him the jobs at the biscuit factory.*"

"*Naturally you did, but he got that job as an assembler, and he earned for nearly two years over £4 a week, did he not?*"

"*Yes, sir, working mechanically.*"

"*What?*"

"*Because he worked mechanically. He never spoke to anyone. He just worked.*"

"*That is true, perhaps, but he was working at piecework as an assembler. It was a well-paid job?*"

"*It was not so well paid. He worked twelve or fourteen hours. In fact, he would have stayed there day and night if he had not been sent home.*"

Evelyn is so proud of her son, even in this courtroom she paints a picture of him as being a hard worker and model employee. She wants to demonstrate the contribution her son has made in civilian life. However, it plays into the hands of Sir Charles and his gameplan. He has done well to coax her into his scenario of Wyeth being 'normal'. He questions Evelyn about the attack on the cyclist, then enquires about how Wyeth got on in borstal and the army. Not once does he mention Wyeth's mental health. For her part, Evelyn continues to perform as the proud mother.

"He got on quite well at borstal, did he not?"

"Yes."

"So well, that they let him out in a year?"

"Yes."

"He had no trouble at all there, did he not?"

"Yes."

"And then he left borstal on the 26th June, 1941?"

"Yes."

"And from July 1941 until May of this year he was in the Pioneer Corps?"

"Yes."

"I think the only trouble he had in the Pioneer Corps was 14 days confined to barracks, was it not?"

"I used to ask him about it, sir, but he never told me."

"*The charge was a very minor one: it was for wetting his bed.*"

"*He had done it from his birth, sir.*"

"*He was there for twelve months, and he only got into this trifling trouble? For that he got fourteen days.*"

"*I knew he could not help it.*"

"*I daresay not. At any rate, that is his record?*"

"*Yes.*"

The final interaction with this defence witness strikes a sympathetic tone. No one in the courtroom can be left with any doubt about Evelyn's love for her adopted son. Perhaps even Sir Charles, in asking her this question, does it in admission of his respect for her.

"*You have been fond of him and extremely kind to him, have you not?*"

Evelyn, without hesitation, responds:

"*Yes, sir.*"

Justice Wrottesley, joins in.

"*You have been a mother to him?*"

For Evelyn, that is all she has ever wanted to be. A mother. Since the death of her baby all those years ago, she has strived to do what she feels is best for her sons. Holding back her emotions, she takes a deep breath before responding.

"Yes, sir. That is why I am here today."

Sir Charles once again offers Evelyn the platform to declare her love for her son. This time his question is in the present tense, not the past tense, perhaps testing her motherly bond in hindsight of what her son is in court for.

"And you are fond of him?"

Without hesitation, and staring straight at her Jim, she replies defiantly.

"Extremely fond of him."

There are no further questions for Evelyn and she is excused from the proceedings. She has done all she can.

MEDICAL EVIDENCE FOR THE DEFENCE

Frank Alpe now calls Dr Louis Rose to the witness stand. The doctor hails from Norwich and is a specialist in mental health, practicing psychiatry and psychotherapy for more than 10 years. The doctor confirms he examined Wyeth at Brixton prison, in June this year, and again at Runwell Hospital, in Essex, just two weeks ago. The doctor has also sat through this trial, so Alpe asks him if he had heard the Chief Inspector's evidence about Wyeth's mother and sister, and the testimony of Evelyn Wyeth. Dr Rose confirms he had. The doctor also states he was already aware of Wyeth's family mental health issues. Alpe asks him to elaborate on what he found when he examined Wyeth in prison.

"On that evidence and on your own examination of him, you have come to some conclusions, I think?"

"Yes, I have."

"I want you to tell my Lord, and the Jury, a little about your examinations of him."

"I saw this man, my Lord, at Brixton prison on the 25th June. I examined him thoroughly physically. I found all his systems, his nervous systems, cardiac system, and intestinal system, those of a healthy man, but he looked anxious and depressed, and, although he was co-operative, all his replies were given in low, monotonous tones. He was anxious and depressed, and only spoke when asked specific questions."

"Did you ask him if he remembered anything about what he had done?"

"He told me a story which was very much the same story I have heard in Court in the last two days, that he remembered seeing this girl, making an excuse to go after her, pulling her down by the back of the coat, and remembered no more until he came to himself and saw her, as he put it, lying on the ground in blood, and then he felt … I have his original words here …he said he grabbed hold of her by the back of the coat,

felt a pain in his head, and then he saw her lying there in a lot of blood. He then seemed to come to his senses, picked something off the ground and flung it over her, went back to camp, and carried on with his work. A few hours later he felt that he had done something wrong, but did not know what it was. He heard some boys talking about a young girl some days later, and realised that he had done it, and was too scared to do anything."

"What was your reaction to that from the way he told you?"

"I believed him."

"Did you ask him if he had any sexual relations with a female?"

"Yes, I did."

"What did he tell you? Tell us about it."

"He told me that he had never experienced any sexual desire or gratification in any form. He had never actually taken out a girl, as far as he says. He has been out with other men to dances, but never actually dances, he stands aside and watches. He told me he had never masturbated, which in a young man I think is abnormal, and, as far as I can gather from his stories of his previous assaults, and things of that kind, he has never experienced any sexual desire or gratification associated with those occurrences."

"I think you took him down to an institution to see if you could detect abnormality with regard to epilepsy?"

"That is so."

"What was that for?"

"The instrument is an electroencephalograph, which is nothing more than a means of amplifying electrical potentials which arise from the skull."

Justice Wrottesley enquires further about the machine. In fact, it is still considered new to medicine. Britain saw its first one in operation in 1935, and at the moment there are just seven units in Britian, operating in specialist psychiatric hospitals. The machine consists of small metal plates which are placed around a person's head to detect electrical pulses within the brain. Those pulses travel through wires to an amplifier and printer to be transformed into waves marked on a roll of paper. At the time, experiments done on patients with epilepsy and those without, showed a real difference in the print-offs between the two. Therefore, for those who advocate the machine, it provides evidence that someone has epilepsy. Most notably, this is the first time the machine has been used as evidence in a British court, and certainly the first time this judge has heard of such a device. For him, it seems like a work of science fiction. The doctor continues.

"The minor abnormalities we found were not sufficient for me to arrive at any conclusion."

If the defence are pinning their hopes on the doctor's testimony, then this is a serious setback. Wrottesley is still getting to grips with the concept of a machine that can map unseen activity within the brain.

"There is a machine by which you get waves which may indicate major or minor epilepsy? But nothing decisive was found?" he asks the doctor. The doctor's response, once again, will not help the defence's cause.

"Nothing decisive enough, my Lord."

Frank Alpe tries to rescue the situation. He asks the doctor if the machine offered the slightest suggestion that Wyeth has epilepsy.

"There were abnormalities present, but those abnormalities do occur in persons other than epileptics, and I do not feel that I could come to any conclusion about it."

"You cannot say from that that he suffered from epilepsy?"

"No."

Alpe enquires about Wyeth's demeanour while being tested. The doctor replies.

"I was a little surprised because he was entirely uninterested in the proceedings. We had to fit electrodes up on springs over his head, he was faced by a tall, rather complicated, electrical

machine, and he lay on a couch submitting to this particular test. I told him there was nothing to be afraid of, that he would not be hurt, that I was trying to discover whether there was anything wrong with his brain. That is, physically. When we had finished the examination he asked no questions, betrayed no interest, simply got up when he was told to and walked off. He had every opportunity, I may say, of talking to me, either confiding or asking questions."

"Having regard to all the evidence before you, including your two examinations of him, will you tell my Lord, and the jury, what conclusions you have come to regarding his state of mind when he committed this act?" Alpe asks.

"My conclusions on my two findings were that this was an abnormal person with an abnormal family history and substandard intelligence. The story of his repeated assaults, as given to me by him and others, was suggestive of some form of post-epileptic or hysterical automatism. I went on to suggest the electro-encephalograph, and finished by saying that there was no ground for suspecting any physical cause for his abnormal behaviour."

Although Dr Rose cannot be sure that Wyeth has epilepsy, he has found evidence to suggest the accused has suffered episodes of unconscious automation, similar to sleepwalking, perhaps even schizophrenia. The judge asks the doctor to confirm that was his conclusion, which he confirms it to be so. Alpe, wanting to exploit the doctor's conclusion further, asks him to elaborate.

"*You told my Lord, and the jury, that when he told you he did not remember doing this thing, but only remembered seeing the little girl there with blood, you believed him.*"

"*By that I meant that such a loss of memory, or such automatism, would be compatible with a person who has exhibited abnormal behaviour, as it has been put to me and as I have found in the various investigations made.*"

"*Will you tell my Lord the opinion you have come to with regard to his mind at the time he committed this act?*"

"*My opinion of that act is that he could not …*"

Wrottesley stops the doctor in mid-sentence. The judge is keen to explore further the state of Wyeth's mind while the act was being done, but the doctor continues to finish what he was about to say.

"*… he could not have known what he was doing.*"

In that sentence the defence have a medical professional stating, without any doubt, that Wyeth was not of sound mind. For Frank Alpe, this is exactly what he wants the jury to hear. He labours the point again with the doctor.

"*Would he know the difference between right and wrong?*"

"*No.*"

The judge intervenes again, asking clarification on a finer point.

"*When you say 'would not', do you mean he did not?*"

"*He did not my Lord*", the doctor replies.

Alpe returns to the discussion.

"*What would that be due to? Not knowing the difference between right and wrong?*"

"*It was due to some form of automatism, some form of maniacal fury, which might be expected in a man with such a history.*"

The judge cannot let that comment go and wants the doctor to elaborate further on what he means.

"*Maniacal fury which might be expected in a man with his history? With what history? What part of his history leads to that?*"

"*A bad family history, an abnormal personal history, and a history of recidivism. A number of assaults for which, as far as I could gather, there was no adequate reason and no adequate satisfaction.*"

Alpe then asks the doctor if he has ever been attacked by one of his patients, a question that infuriates the judge, who cannot see the point in the question. But Alpe wants to explore what the doctor saw, in terms of the violent patient's behaviour, immediately following the attack.

The judge denies the defence question, this case is about Wyeth, not observations on other patients. The judge, in front of the court, scolds the barrister like a school teacher confronting a naughty pupil.

"*This gentleman is here to give an opinion, is he not?*"

"*Yes, my Lord.*" Alpe replies.

"*On facts which in this case happen to be pretty well not in dispute.*"

"*No, my Lord.*"

With that, the defence declare they have finished questioning their witness. They hand the floor over to Sir Charles, who is keen to dismiss any notion that Wyeth was unaware of his actions. The prosecution barrister refers Dr Rose to Wyeth's attack on the cyclist. The doctor declares he had been informed of that incident, so Sir Charles asks if the doctor sought any evidence of unconscious automation linked to Wyeth's actions in it. The doctor confirms he had. Sir Charles now goes on the offensive.

"*Do you know that he was lying alongside the girl in a ditch, and that she said, he said to her, according to her evidence, don't make a fuss, I only want to seduce you?*"

"*I have not heard that before.*"

"*You have never heard that?*"

"*No.*"

"*Is that not a very important matter if you are judging a man's mental condition?*"

"*Yes.*"

"*If a man said that, lying alongside of, and struggling with, a girl, intending to seduce her by force, that does not indicate automatism, does it?*"

"*By no means.*"

"*It is criminal, but perfectly sane?*"

"*Yes.*"

Frank Alpe is outraged. Moments ago, he was scolded for referring to an event outside the remit of this hearing, with the judge making it clear the witness can only offer an opinion on the facts of this case. Yet, just now, the prosecution has sought a doctor's opinion on Wyeth's state of mind in a previous attack, despite the doctor not being directly involved with the case at the time. Dr Rose's admission that Wyeth's actions back then were those of a sane man will have undermined all the science the defence brought to court. Alpe questions the judge as to why it is allowed. Wrottesley responds, although his justification for allowing it is somewhat ambiguous. He explains:

"*He is not asked whether it is a fact. He is asked whether he would agree that if that were the fact, he would not call it automatism. This witness' evidence is that this man had never had anything in the shape of sexual desire or sexual satisfaction."*

Sir Charles continues his questioning of the doctor. He moves on from the previous attack and wants to know the doctor's opinions on Wyeth's state of mind when the accused stalked Pat on Riddlesworth Park that fateful morning. In doing so, he will show Wyeth had made up his mind to attack the girl before carrying out the deed, even if the accused claims he was not aware while he was doing it.

"I want to know exactly when you think this maniacal state of fury starts. It does not start when he sees the little girl walking down the path, does it?"

"No."

"It does not start when he makes an excuse by which he is able to get away from his work?"

"No."

"He follows her along the path and overtakes her, grabs her, as we have heard, but the back of the neck, and drags her into the bushes?"

"Yes."

"There is no evidence there of any maniacal fury, is there?"

"No."

"It is extremely possible, although there is no evidence of it, I agree, that the girl would scream, if she could scream, if he had not got her too tightly by the throat?"

"It is likely."

"Is it not also extremely probable that he was banging her head on the ground to silence her screaming?"

"I doubt that."

"There were injuries to the mouth and eyes, apparently caused by his hands – very severe injuries to the head. You know the evidence?"

"I have heard the evidence."

"It is more likely is it not, if the girl is injured by having her head banged on the ground several times, that it is done for the simple reason of silencing her?"

"I am not prepared to answer that question."

"You mean it may be so or it may not?"

"Yes."

"Do you think that if he was banging her head on the ground to silence her, that was maniacal?"

"I think the whole of that episode must have been maniacal, judging from the photographs of the injuries I have seen."

"*The fact that he took her into the bushes shows that whatever his fury was when he was dragging her by the neck, he had the intelligence to take her somewhere where he could not be seen?*"

"*Yes.*"

Sir Charles is shepherding the defence's own witness to slowly peel apart the defence argument. He has now demonstrated to the jury that Wyeth's actions were those of someone calculating their next move, rather than simply going through unconscious emotions. Wrottesley joins in, his interrogation more confirming this fact than questioning it.

"*That shows calculation, does it not? Taking her away where she could not be seen, under the trees, in order to do what he was going to do?*"

"*Yes.*"

"*That shows intelligence, does it not?*"

"*Yes.*"

"*It does not show mania?*"

"*I am referring to the incidents which occur after the dragging.*"

"*The fact that he covers over the body with a piece of sacking which he finds nearby shows intelligence, does it not?*"

274

"*Yes.*"

"*So, at any rate he knew what he was doing, and was acting intelligently, up to the moment when he got to the bushes?*"

"*Yes.*"

Mr Alpe must know this is a huge setback. Dr Rose has just admitted that Wyeth's alleged lack of memory likely occurred after the attack but not during it, perhaps erasing thoughts of what had happened. It implies Wyeth had full control of his mind when he attacked Pat. Right now, more than at any other time, Wyeth is a condemned man. Nonetheless, Sir Charles adds another dimension to the attack, one which society finds abhorrent on a girl of such a young age.

"*Whatever that impulse was, it was wholly consistent with the purpose for which he had left his work first of all, sexual gratification with this little girl at some time. It is consistent with that, is it not?*"

"*Yes.*"

Justice Wrottesley asks a couple of questions on this matter. In doing so, he underlines Sir Charles' recent approach.

"*The evidence is that the girl was half naked?*"

"*Yes.*"

"That looks like sexual behaviour, does it not?"

"Yes."

The prosecution, having made their point succinctly, retire from asking further questions. Frank Alpe receives approval from the judge to re-examine his witness, in anticipation he can salvage something from this debacle.

"In mental cases, it is sometimes found that the patient realises having done something wrong after it is done, remembers nothing about the incident?"

Wrottesley takes issue with the manner of this question. In a trial laden with leading questions, he objects to Alpe's latest one. The judge re-phrases the barrister's words to question when someone does not know what they are doing, they might still comprehend it is wrong to act in such a way. The doctor is hesitant to commit either way with an answer, but the judge reminds him he has sworn an oath to answer honestly, and anyway the jury need to hear it. The doctor, however, refuses to be drawn on giving his opinion. Ultimately, the judge backs down and Alpe resumes his questions. Ironically, his next question is similar to the one the judge struck out just minutes ago. This time it is not challenged.

"Have you known an attack to be made upon someone else by a mental person?"

"*Yes.*"

"*What has happened afterwards? Has the patient known he has done it?*"

"*On a large number of occasions, they know what they have done, and often apologise for it.*"

"*They know afterwards?*"

"*Yes.*"

"*I think you have been laid out after being hit, have you not?*"

"*Yes.*"

"*What happened afterwards?*"

"*One particular man had a blackout lasting about half a minute. He was helped to a bed, and was told afterwards, almost immediately, that he had hit me, and was very grieved about it and apologetic. He did not remember doing it.*"

Although this time the doctor was able to respond to Alpe's question about being personally attacked, Justice Wrottesley again takes issue with the barrister's approach and questions the relevance of what is being said. Alpe, now feeling frustrated at being constantly shut down by the judge, turns to Dr Rose to reignite the discussion about patients not being able to restrain themselves from violent acts and apologising later. The barrister suggests to the doctor that he was then about to tell the jury this, but the judge is not having his authority here challenged in such a manner. His word is final, so he reprimands Alpe again for trying to put words into the mouth of a witness. The barrister takes a moment to gather his thoughts and consider a different plan of attack. He knows he is thin on options, what with the judge constantly closing him down, so he approaches the doctor again.

"From all the facts in this history, the fury of the attack, and all the information you have got from the witness here, you have come to a definite conclusion, have you not?"

"Yes."

"Which you have told the jury?"

"Yes."

Alpe will not lead the witness any further and declares to the judge he has finished with his questions. Has he salvaged anything? He is not sure. Wrottesley wants to clarify a few points with Dr Rose before the witness is released from court. Alpe may feel some justification that the questions asked by the judge could be objected to on similar grounds that his were, that of conjecture.

"You told us that you asked him for an account which he gave you, an account that was very similar to that read to the jury, that he did not know anything about it when he did it.

You told us that you accepted that."

"Yes."

"Sometimes these people very often do not tell the truth? Like other people?"

"Yes."

"Supposing you had not believed what he told you when he told you that, would you have come to the same conclusion? Is it one of the things which led you to come to the conclusion that he did not know what he was doing and did not know the difference between right and wrong?"

"I think in the first place I believed him because his attitude and general story fitted in …"

"I did not ask you that! What I am asking you specifically is: If you had not believed him and thought he was lying to you and hiding away what he knew, would you still have come to the same conclusion?"

"I do not think I could have, my Lord."

"I thought not, but I wanted to be sure."

Dr Rose has perhaps endured the most robust cross-examination of all the witnesses. He has brought modern science to the courtroom and been asked for his opinion, but equally shut down when offering it. His grilling is complete when the judge suggests he must surely know of the M'Naghten Rule. The doctor confirms he does and is then dismissed. Despite most of the courtroom not knowing what the M'Naghten Rule means, it is not expanded upon. For those practising law they will be aware it dates back a hundred years, following the acquittal, on grounds of insanity, of a man accused of the assassination of a British Prime Minister's secretary. Following that murder trial, guidelines were issued for courts when considering a plea of insanity.

"… *the jurors ought to be told that every man is to be presumed to be sane, and to possess a sufficient degree of reason to be responsible for his crimes, until the contrary be proved to their satisfaction. And that to establish a defence on the ground of insanity, it must be clearly proved that, at the time of the committing of the act, the party accused was labouring under such a defect of reason, from disease of the mind, as not to know the nature and quality of the act he was doing. Or, if he did know it, that he did not know he was doing what was wrong.*"

Frank Alpe, perhaps already feeling defeated, turns to the judge.

"*That is the case for the defence, my Lord.*"

A LAST-MINUTE ADDITION

During the cross-examination of Evelyn Wyeth, attention was drawn to a psychology report on her 'Jim', collated by Dr Grierson, the doctor at Brixton prison. The report brought together the professional opinions of all those who examined Wyeth while he was in prison and it was released only the day before the trial began, so it has not been formally included in the list of evidence. It seems the report's conclusion was that Wyeth has been untruthful about blacking out when attacking Pat, which may be why the defence omitted to make it a last-minute addition to their case. However, during Evelyn's time in the witness stand, Sir Charles told the judge about it and he in turn requested it be brought to the attention of the jury. Now, after both the prosecution and the defence have finished calling their witnesses, Sir Charles approaches the judge and requests to bring Dr Grierson to the proceedings. The doctor has made the half-hour journey from Brixton prison to the Old Bailey, to wait in the corridor adjacent to the courtroom. The judge authorises this addition, so the doctor is summoned and enters the room. He walks to the witness stand.

The clerk of the court swears in Dr Grierson and it is Sir Charles who is the first to question the doctor, implying the witness is for the prosecution. The barrister asks background questions about the doctor's involvement with Wyeth. The doctor informs the court he had seen the accused in person on many occasions and has pooled together reports from other staff. Sir Charles' questions slowly dismantle the defence's theory that Wyeth was insane when attacking Pat.

"*I think you obtained no history of fits or of insanity in the accused himself?*"

"*That is so.*"

"*Do you know the circumstances of the assault which led to him being sent to borstal?*"

"*Yes.*"

"*In those matters do you find any evidence of any automatism or maniacal fury?*"

"*No.*"

"*He went, I think, with your knowledge and approval, at any rate with your knowledge and permission, to the Sutton Emergency Hospital, where an electro encephalographic record was made?*"

"*Yes.*"

"*As no result has come from that, I need not ask you more than this – I think that is a form of science which is supposed to be quite in its infancy is it not?*"

"*Yes.*"

"*Whatever its result had been, would you attach any real importance to it?*"

"*I have no experience of it myself. I'm only going on what an expert on the matter told me about it.*"

"*Whilst the prisoner has been under your care has he eaten and slept well?*"

"*Yes, he has.*"

"*Will you tell us generally the result of your observations of him?*"

"*Do you want my final conclusion?*"

"*I think you may give a little more detail as to the result of your observations.*"

"*In the ward he has kept mostly to himself, reading, and had little to do with the other inmates. At interviews he has shown mostly a passive attitude, being a person of few words, and usually speaks only when spoken to. That attitude is, I think, due to an introverted state rather than to indolence.*"

Wrottesley asks Dr Grierson to clarify what he meant about the accused's attitude. The doctor's response is a lengthy one:

"*A man in an introverted state is a man whose mind is turned on himself, turned inwards instead of outwards. He*" *stated that he had had blackouts or black fits in the past, but when I examined him on those, I could obtain no definite instances. All that he would say was that he forgot for a time where he was when he brooded at home. His past history of assaults on girls is in line with the present charge. I noticed that in 1940, when convicted on his own plea of such an assault, he alleged he did not remember all that had happened. He now states that his memory returned later. As to the present charge, he repeats what he had already said to the police in exhibit eleven, that in his statement he did not remember what happened after dragging the girl under the trees. The period of this alleged loss of memory covers that in which the alleged murder was supposedly committed. Beyond his own statement I find no further evidence of any mental disease or disorder with which a loss of memory might be associated."*

Based on Dr Grierson's testimony, the jury will cast away any notion of Wyeth not knowing what he was doing. Here, before them, a picture is being painted of the accused calculating his every move. The judge wants to be absolutely sure that there was no mental disease reported while Wyeth was in Brixton prison. He asks the doctor:

"There are such mental diseases or disorders, are there not?"

"*Yes,*" the doctor replies.

"*But did you not find any such diseases in this case?*"

"*I did not my Lord.*"

Sir Charles resumes his questions.

"*I think you subjected him to certain intelligence tests?*"

"*Yes.*"

"*What was the result?*"

"*He was only just a little below normal, it was not very much.*"

"*What is your conclusion from that?*"

"*I think he is a person of the introverted and solitary type. I am not satisfied that his alleged loss of memory is genuine. I have not found signs of any mental disease which would influence my opinion and prevent him knowing what he was doing was wrong.*"

"*So, he did know what he was doing, in your opinion, and he knew what was wrong?*"

"*In my opinion, yes.*"

Sir Charles announces to the court that he has copies of Dr Grierson's report. Frank Alpe is handed a copy, as is the judge, and the doctor too. The doctor, after reading it, confirms it is an exact copy of what he wrote. Alpe steps forward to ask the doctor about his report.

"Does not that report say that he was abnormal in borstal, that he had abnormalities in borstal?"

"Yes, I think this man is to a certain extent abnormal."

"Does not that report that has just been handed to us bear out the evidence of Dr Rose?"

Wrottesley does not allow the doctor to answer and instead objects to the question. The judge requests Alpe to be more specific about the content of both reports. The defence barrister re-phrases his question, but the doctor denies both reports are compatible. Dr Grierson tells Alpe that Dr Rose was treating Wyeth for epilepsy but this was not something considered while the accused was in Brixton prison. Alpe turns his attention to the last paragraph of the report, which reads: "I came to regard him towards the end of the first twelve months as a person with a psychopathic personality."

Dr Grierson is again non-committal in his reply.

"That does not necessarily mean hysteria."

Alpe continues his questions.

"It showed that his mental condition was called in question then?"

"Yes, his psychological condition."

"Taking that with the evidence of Mrs Wyeth of the

abnormalities when he was a child, does not that point to a general mental condition?"

"I say I think he is an abnormal type of person."

"His half-sister is in a mental hospital?"

"Yes."

"His mother's sister is detained in a mental institution for violent mental cases?"

"Brampton is a state institution for those with violent or criminal propensities and unfit ..."

"Does not that help you come to a conclusion?"

Yet again, Wrottesley is outraged by the manner of Alpe's questioning. He demands Alpe not interrupt the witness, then invites the doctor to finish his answer. Dr Grierson takes a second, then speaks.

"The type of person who is unfit to associate with non-criminals, which may be from many points of view. They may not be all violent. They may be sexual."

"Isn't that mental?"

"Yes."

"Doesn't that make you come to the conclusion that Dr Rose is right?"

"The family history is of assistance when one finds that it is confirmatory evidence of mental disease or disorder in the

family, but in the examination of any single person it depends whether you find any mental disease or disorder in that person himself. The mere family history in itself is not sufficient to show that a person is of unsound mind."

"*I mean all the points put together.*"

"*It points to it being in the family.*"

"*It confirms it?*"

"*It helps to confirm it.*"

It appears Dr Grierson is never going to agree with Alpe's suggestions. Alpe then refers to the episode when Wyeth rode a pony at a girl. He questions the doctor as to whether that could be considered an abnormal act. Again, the doctor will not commit either way to an answer, instead he suggests he needs more information to make his mind up. Alpe tries another question. Is it normal for a boy to take a child into a field? Dr Grierson admits that is not the action of a well-behaved boy, however, purely being abnormal does not mean the boy is insane or suffering from a mental illness. Alpe is getting nowhere, so he finishes his questions.

Sir Charles steps back onto the floor and questions the witness a final time. He asks the doctor if mental illness can be hereditary, aiming to demonstrate that the mental health of Wyeth's family should have no bearing on Wyeth's own mental health.

"With regard to the family history, is it unusual, with people who appear to be in a very humble walk of life, that one out of nine should be mentally defective?"

"It is not unusual, no."

"The other eight appear to have no history of mental deficiency?"

"It is not unusual. On the other hand, you may get a family of thirteen or fourteen, and find none of them mentally deficient."

"At any rate, with regard to this boy you find, do you not, no disease of the mind or defect of reason?"

"That is so."

The witness is about to be dismissed, but Frank Alpe approaches the judge beforehand. Alpe suggests Sir Charles' example of nine children, with one having a mental disease, relates specifically to Wyeth's family. Alpe outlines his concerns, by suggesting the doctor, if referring to Wyeth's family, made a generalisation when giving his assessment because the doctor knows nothing of the specifics of the family, what with only having medically assessed the accused. In Alpe's mind, such generalisations have seen himself shut down repeatedly by the judge. However, Alpe may have an ulterior motive for asking this question. Although it looks like this trial is decided upon, he may have one eye on a subsequent appeal. He invites the judge to comment.

"*Would your Lordship allow me to ask one question? My learned friend just put something about abnormality in one out of nine. I understood from the evidence the other eight could not be traced. He does not know anything about them.*"

Wrottesley responds abruptly. Looking down upon Alpe, he tells the barrister that the doctor had already replied to the question.

"*No, he was really asked, 'Was the fact that one out of nine suffered from mental defect unusual?' And the answer was no.*"

Then, without allowing a response from Alpe, Wrottesley thanks the doctor and dismisses him from the proceedings. The defence barrister gives a sigh. Not loud enough for the judge to hear, but enough for himself to express his own frustration at his treatment in court. After the witness has left, Alpe lifts his head to look at the judge. He offers his summary of his case to the courtroom.

"*Members of the jury, I am going to address you shortly now, on behalf of this accused man. As I told you when I opened this case to you, the verdict that I and my learned friend, acting as we do for the Defence, ask you to return a verdict of guilty but insane. If you do return that verdict, you need not be frightened or alarmed that this man will be let loose on society. There is no fear of that. In fact, one feels like congratulating Chief Inspector Barrett and Inspector Garner, of the Norfolk Constabulary, for sifting out from all these soldiers, this man who did this terrible deed.*

I want you to consider for a few moments one fact. What would you think, supposing you had heard that some man had committed a crime of this nature? Inflicted these terrible wounds on a harmless little child? Apparently without any reason, as far as we can see from the evidence that has been produced before you, because Dr Webster said, and he made the most careful post-mortem examination, that there was no attempt at sexual interference with this child whatsoever.

When I put it to Dr Walton that it was like the work of a maniac, he said, 'Yes'. Then he went on to say, 'He carried her into the bushes'. My answer to that is – so does a wild beast without any understanding. If this was not the work of a maniac, what is? Banging her head on the ground? What for? My learned friend said, 'To stifle her cries'. One would have thought that the instrument was enough to do that. The accused man was banging her head on the ground, members of the jury, so violently that he made a large indent, as the police have given evidence. There were nail marks on the poor little child's head, and something more important members of the jury, than that, the instrument was inserted here." The defence barrister points to under his chin, then continues:

"... and went through the little child's mouth. Dr Webster told you it was not just pushed in and pulled out. It was pushed in and wriggled about. What for? Was that to stifle her cries?

I am not going through the various wounds inflicted on this poor, innocent child. The stab wounds, the ear partly cut off, strangulation, and the banging of the head. I am not going to ask you to consider that alone. I asked for those photographs to be put in, and I asked my learned friend to put them in, because I wanted you to see them. You have looked at them. That is enough. One's feelings are quite sufficiently harrowed in this case without looking any more at those photographs, but they do show you something of the hurt that this man, whom my learned friend says is a little abnormal, because that is the evidence, inflicted on this child for no reason. Apparently. Jealousy, passion, greed, lust, revenge, are surely all absent. If you have heard that those wounds had been inflicted on a little child, and some man you knew, or some friend of yours, had done it, would you not have come to the conclusion that he must have been mad?

I want you to go back to the time when, as a little child, this man was abandoned and taken into the care of that lady who gave evidence, who was then living in Wales. Mrs Wyeth. Dr Grierson said, 'Oh, yes, there is some abnormality'. It started very young, did it not? When he saw a man, even his adopted father, he used to shriek quite loudly, according to

Mrs Wyeth. It took him 12 months to get used to the man he saw every night, who had then become his father. For a year he used to shriek every time he saw him. Then there was the late talking. You would expect a little child of three or four years of age to be anxious to play with other children? No. He never played with other children. Then we come to later on in life, charging this pony at a little girl and threatening to put a little girl in the river.

Members of the jury, I do not know whether his condition may have been progressive or not, but we do know this, that when he was in borstal, they had some doubt about his mental condition. Dr Rose was honestly trying to do his best not to exaggerate, but to give his evidence in a detached manner. He is a doctor of some experience, who knows something about mental cases. He is a mental specialist attached to mental hospitals. Dr Rose said, 'In my opinion, taking all his earlier history, my interview with him, his detached and unconcerned attitude regarding that examination which was made at the hospital, I have come to the conclusion, having regard to the maniacal attack, the terrible attack, and the terrible injuries, that he did not know what he was doing at the time. He did not know he was doing wrong'. I invite you to say, members of the jury, that his violent outburst was not only due to defect of reason, but to defect of reason due to disease of the mind. Because if he did not know what he was doing and did not know it was wrong, in my submission you should come to the *conclusion, if you accept it, that his mind was affected.*

The facts are all before you. You have listened so carefully to all the evidence that it is not necessary for me to go over it all again. I am only going to say this to you now. Consider his early history. Consider the terrible injuries inflicted on this harmless, poor little girl. You must come to the one conclusion that it was the work of a madman, because, apparently, there was no satisfaction to anybody in this dreadful attack.

I am going to ask you once again, and I am going to repeat what I said to you. When you consider your verdict, to take yourselves away from the atmosphere of this Court, if you can, and consider all the evidence. Consider it with the same common sense, may I say, with the same reasoning, that you would bring to bear on your ordinary everyday workday life. You will come to only one conclusion. That the Defence has satisfied you, that at the time this man did this act he did not know what he was doing. That he did not know he was doing wrong. And that it was through defect of the mind that he did it.

Members of the jury. I leave the matter in your hands."

Although the prosecution has already given their closing speech, Justice Wrottesley asks Sir Charles if he wishes to address the jury one last time. Sir Charles declines, probably believing he has won over the jury already so there is no point endangering that advantage.

For the jury's benefit, the judge sums up the case. It is a lengthy summary, one where we can see the verdict he is directing the jury towards. He begins:

"*Now, members of the jury, the case is going to pass into your hands. It now appears there is not the least doubt that the accused man committed this terrible and horrible crime which is charged against him. That morning, the little girl left her foster mother, who was looking after her, to go to school across that park. She never got there at all. She was pursued and overtaken by the accused, who dragged her out of sight, under those trees, and subjected her to treatment from which she died.*

Now that you know all about it, and have been told everything that anybody can find about it, upon those facts the only question for you, is whether the proper verdict is that the accused man is guilty of murder, or whether the proper verdict is that he was guilty of the act but insane at the time he did it.

It is my duty to tell you, that in this country, all persons are presumed to be sane until the contrary is shown. You and I are to be taken to know what will follow, as the results of our acts. If we take a knife or some other instrument and push it into a child's head and neck, that child is likely to die, and the result is murder.

There are certain circumstances in which it is upon the

defence to discharge that presumption, and to satisfy the jury by material evidence put before the jury, that that principle does not apply in any particular case. That is the burden which the defence have taken upon themselves in this case. They have just been asking you through Counsel to say that this young man was insane at the time he did this, and insane so as not to be responsible for his actions.

The evidence upon which that can be established to your satisfaction can, of course, be, as it has been, put on two grounds. You can be told facts from which you, members of the jury, may, if you like, infer sanity or insanity. It is usual now, it has happened in this case, to assist the jury by calling medical evidence.

I wish to safeguard you against thinking this – that if a crime is sufficiently horrible, that you are driven to assume that the person who did it cannot be sane. That is a dangerous and wrong line of reasoning. If that line of reasoning were to be followed, it would be sufficient that one of us could commit a sufficiently horrible crime and a jury would be asked to say from that alone that the prisoner cannot have been sane.

You and I know, that the impulses to which human nature is liable may include horrible, beastly, cruel impulses. It is the duty of all of us to resist an evil impulse. The fact that a person does not resist a wrong impulse is not insanity, for the criminal courts of this country could go out of work. That is not the way in which these matters should be approached. The question you have to make up your minds about is: Was the accused person responsible for what he did? He or she is responsible unless certain things are made out to your satisfaction. I will tell you what they are.

First of all, in order that a person may escape, and be held not responsible for some wrong or horrible deed like this, which he or she has done, the first thing to be established, before you can bring in a verdict of guilty of the act but insane when he or she did it, is that there must be mental illness. Mental disease. That is the first thing. And that is not enough. It must be mental disease of a certain kind. It must be a mental disease or disorder which results in faulty reasoning. A defect of reasoning. That is to say, that the person in question does not reason as you or I would, but reasons wrongly in this way. That he does not know the nature of the wrongful act that he does. Let me give you an instance. A person who is in a state of mania, cases are known of course, I daresay you have seen them, such a state of mania that obviously he does not know any different. Put a knife or sword into the hands of such a person and it is clear that in a fit of mania somebody may be killed. You would rightly, in a case like that, say, 'Here is a case of a person suffering from mental disease which led to such defective and faulty state of reasoning that the person did not know what he was doing at all'. That is a clear case where you would rightly say, 'We shall not hold the person in *question responsible for the killing of any person who may be killed in a fit of that kind.' That is one simple case.*

Another case is this. That this mental disease, if you find there is this mental disease, has created such a defect of reasoning of this kind, that the perpetrator of the deed did not know that it was wrong. Let me put an extreme case of that kind. We all know of, or have heard of, people who suffer hallucinations. Supposing it was such an hallucination as to make him believe his best friend was, let us say, an enemy. That, to you, might seem to justify him in falling upon that person and killing him.

I put before you, simple cases in order that you may see the line of reasoning you should adopt in this case. Bearing that in mind, and bearing in mind this case, it being plain now that this young man took that child that day and treated her in the way he did. If you are to do as Counsel asks you to do, and bring in a verdict that he did the act but was insane at the time that he did it, you must remember the evidence which has been called upon in this matter. It is not, as I have indicated, enough to say, 'It is impossible to think that any decent man could have done such a thing'. That is not enough. Unfortunately, decent men do such things. The evidence is the medical evidence. It is not enough that he should be abnormal. Members of the jury, there are plenty of abnormal persons in the world, and it would be a bad day for this country, were it to go forth that abnormal persons could go and commit any crimes because juries would be told they are abnormal and therefore cannot be punished. That clearly will not do, and does not make sense. The question is, did he know that what he was doing was wrong?

What is the evidence? You have had called before you professional men on either hand. First of all, Dr Louis Rose, who told you that he examined this man twice. He got hold of his life history and the history of his family. That was quite right. They are all materials such a doctor ought to have before him if he is to come to a sound conclusion on a matter of this kind. He questioned this young man about this case. He told you the story which was read to you today, namely, that he dragged the child behind the trees, in itself a wrongful act, and when he got her there, he did not know what he did until he came-to and found the young child lying in front of him bathed in her own blood. Or words to that effect. The doctor said he believed him, and the conclusion to which he came was that he was an abnormal person with an abnormal history.

Members of the jury. As I say, that is not really the point. We have not reached a point where it is enough to tell a jury that a person is abnormal and cannot therefore be held responsible for what he does. Dr Rose went on to say that this man had substandard intelligence. That is not enough. Stupidity is no excuse for a crime of this kind. Being backward mentally, is not an excuse for a crime of this kind. He said,

'The previous assaults suggested some form of hysterical automatism. There is no physical cause for his abnormal behaviour, and that is my conclusion as to his mental state.' Then he was asked questions by Counsel for the accused, and he said originally, 'When he committed the act, he could not know what he was doing'. But later on, he said that he ought to say, 'He did not know what he was doing', and then went on to say, 'He did not know the difference between right and wrong. Some form of automatism took place, some maniacal fury such as was to be expected in a man with his history'. Then he told you that he would not have come to that conclusion unless he believed what the man told him as to not remembering what took place. That was the evidence of Dr Rose, who studies these questions.

Then for your assistance, there was called Dr Grierson, the senior medical officer at Brixton prison. He must have, perhaps, a unique experience in examining into the mental state of people. Particularly people who come before criminal courts. He has had the accused under observation. He has had him in the hospital ward from the sixteenth of last month, up to the present time. He has had before him all this material. Some of which was put before you, including that report from borstal, where he was when he got into trouble over this girl whom he indecently assaulted. He had seen him, and spoken to him, and conversed with him, and studied the case.

I need not repeat in detail the grounds upon which he

based his opinion. The gist of his opinion is this, 'Whilst under my care he was eating and sleeping normally. In the ward he has kept mostly to himself, reading, having little to do with the other inmates. He adopts a passive attitude at interviews, being a man of few words. He said he had blackouts in the past, but when examined could not give definite instances. His past history of assaults on girls is in line with the present charge. In 1940, when he was convicted on his own plea, in relation to an assault on a girl, he said he did not remember all that had happened.'

He repeated to Dr Grierson the same account of this tragic occurrence as he gave to Dr Rose. Dr Grierson said he could find no further evidence of mental disease or disorder with which loss of memory might be associated. Dr Grierson could find no trace of such incidents in this case. He said he is only slightly subnormal from the point of view of intelligence. The opinion of Dr Grierson is that he is not satisfied that his alleged loss of memory on this occasion is genuine, and he has found no sign of mental disease, which would, in the opinion of Dr Grierson, prevent him from knowing what he was doing, or prevent him from knowing that what he did was wrong.

There are the two options. On the other hand, there is also, and you will take this into your consideration, the evidence of what took place. He himself says that from the moment he dragged the child under the tree he knew nothing. Against that there is the fact that he concealed her, and he made plans by which he could follow and overtake the girl, and he made plans by which he could get back.

All those are matters for you to consider. Those may seem to you to be matters which are more in accordance with this man being responsible. You have to remember this. You will be bound to find this person guilty of murder unless you are satisfied that at the time he was suffering from a disease of the mind, that that brought about a defect of reasoning, faulty reasoning, and that as a result of that, one or two things happened. Either that he did not know what he was doing. Or that, even if he did know what he was doing, he did not know it was wrong.

I will say that once more. One of two things. First of all, mental disease. Secondly, faulty reasoning. That is to say, not reasoning as you or I do, and faulty reasoning of such a kind that he either did not know what he was doing when he killed the child or that when he killed the child, he thought he was doing right. I see no trace at all of any suggestion that the latter applies. So really it is upon the former that you should concentrate. Are you satisfied that, when he did that, it was a result of mental disease and he did not know what he was doing? Unless you are satisfied in that, you will, in accordance with the evidence, say that he is guilty of murder.

Will you now consider your verdict."

THE VERDICT

The jury members are dismissed and proceedings adjourned until they have reached their verdict. The clerk records the time as being 2.48pm. The judge, barristers and many of the court officials retire from proceedings during this time. Members of the public gallery take this opportunity to quickly nip off to the toilet, or to simply stretch their legs. It is not long before the courtroom is called back, it seems the jury do not need much time to deliberate and come to a conclusion. Everyone returns to the courtroom to take up their seats. The time is recorded as being 3.35pm. The room is now hushed to silence. With an air of expectation, the clerk of the court asks the foreman of the jury to stand and speak on behalf of the other jurors. The clerk then directs this question to him:

"Members of the jury, are you agreed upon your verdict?"

The foreman speaks.

"We are."

"Do you find the prisoner, James Wyeth, guilty or not guilty of murder?"

"Guilty of murder."

Although the verdict was expected, there are audible gasps from the public gallery. Some of the gallery express pleasure at the verdict, releasing a cheer. They feel it's a just verdict against a vicious child killer, in a world that has no place for such a monster. Lost among the gasps and cheers is the sad emotion expressed by a mother whose son has just been convicted. The Clerk continues the formalities.

"You find him guilty of murder and that is the verdict of you all?"

"It is."

None of the jury bought into the defence premise that Wyeth was insane when he attacked Pat. Without exception, their belief is that Wyeth carried out a cold and callous act of murder upon an innocent and defenceless six-year-old girl who was simply walking to school. Through all this trial, and throughout the verdict of the jury, Wyeth has sat, void of emotion. Apart from being asked if he was guilty, at the commencement of the hearing, he has been excluded from the proceedings. Barristers and witnesses have talked about him, as though he was not in the room. To be fair, for the most part, his expression has signified that his mind was in fact that, namely not in the room. The Clerk of the Court, now addresses Wyeth:

"Prisoner at the bar, you stand convicted of murder. Have you anything to say why the Court should not give you judgement of death, according to law?"

Wyeth says nothing. He offers a slight shake of the head, but betrays no emotion. No facial expression. Nothing.

All that is left now, is for Justice Wrottesley to pass sentence. He has no room for leniency. This is a capital crime and a most heinous one at that. He solemnly looks at Wyeth, with the prisoner simply bowing his head and shutting his eyes while the judge reads the sentence…

"The sentence of the Court is that laid down by law, which is, that you be taken from here to the place from where you came, and from there to a place of execution, where you shall be hanged by the neck until you are dead."

BREAKING NEWS

Newspaper reporters rush their stories to their editors, hoping to have it included in the late afternoon editions, thus being among the first to break news …

Birmingham Mail – *Wyeth was found guilty of murder and sentenced to death.*

Leicester Daily Mercury – *Pioneer to die for child murder. At the Old Bailey James Wyeth (22), private in the Pioneer Corps, was found guilty of the murder of Patricia Ann Cupit, a six-year-old London evacuee, at Thetford, Norfolk, and was sentenced to death.*

Yorkshire Evening Post – *Murdered child evacuee. Death sentence on soldier.*

PART FOUR – THE LEGAL AFTERMATH
SATURDAY, 18ᵀᴴ JULY, 1942

Morning Advertiser – *Skull waves test in murder case. A test with an electric instrument which records "skull waves", was described at the Old Bailey yesterday, when James Wyeth, 22, soldier, was sentenced to death for the murder of Patricia Ann Cupit, aged 6. The defence had asked for a verdict of "guilty, but insane". A doctor said that Wyeth had been tested with an electric encephalograph, and instrument which recorded 'skull waves', which might indicate major or minor epilepsies.*

Following the conclusion of James Wyeth's trial, the authorities have certain formalities to carry out. Firstly, he was immediately taken from the Old Bailey and returned to Norwich prison. Upon receiving Wyeth, the Norwich prison governor makes a note in his journal,

"Received J Wyeth at 8.45pm today on a sentence of death."

Prior to the trial, Wyeth would have been monitored as much as any other prisoner in Norwich. Then, upon questions over the prisoner's mental state, he was sent to Brixton for assessment. Now Wyeth has returned to Norfolk, following his conviction, with questions raised about his mental state, the governor informs his medical officer that, in no uncertain terms, it is the medical officer who must personally oversee every observation of

Wyeth's mental and physical condition. This request is above and beyond the normal day-to-day prison routine, seemingly a humane one. However, the Secretary of State is getting involved in Wyeth's case, hinting he may enquire about such observations if he feels compelled to examine the case in more depth. There is also another reason. It will allow the prison to better prepare Wyeth for execution if they note the man becomes distressed at the prospect of his imminent demise.

Wyeth is housed in a cell, away from the main prison, specifically set aside for those sentenced to death, although it is rarely required. The cell is close enough to the room housing the gallows, so Wyeth will not have to walk in full view of other prisoners on the day of execution, but it is just far enough away that he will not hear the preparations and rehearsals taking place. Even though Norwich prison has seen a few executions over the years, every execution will be different. Every execution has a strict protocol to follow. The trap door is checked to make sure it will not malfunction. The prisoner's height is considered for the noose and their weight is replicated in the rehearsals by bags of ballast. Get the weight wrong on the day and the noose may rise up the neck to prevent a clean kill. It may even go the other way and rip through the neck. It is at Norwich prison where his execution is to be carried out, with a provisional time and date being 9am, on Tuesday 4th August 1942.

The governor issues strict guidelines for the inmates' routines for the day of execution. He states they will not be allowed to congregate in groups, instead, they are to be scattered around the prison and given tasks to occupy their minds. Those who would normally exercise in the yard, which is near the room housing the gallows, will instead take exercise elsewhere. The governor also requests the chimes on the prison clock are to be silenced that morning, so the prisoners will not know for sure when the hanging takes place. All these precautions are for the benefit of the prisoners, especially the younger ones, who may become unsettled if their focus is on an execution being carried out in the prison.

Albert Pierrepoint has been nominated as the principal hangman to carry out Wyeth's death sentence. Pierrepoint will later become Britain's most prolific hangman of the 20th century, executing 434 men and women, in a 23-year career, 156 of them convicted Nazi war criminals after the war. But for now, for the past ten years, he has mainly assisted with executions across the country, building up his experience, until last year when he became a principal executioner. In a widely reported execution just last month, at Wandsworth prison, he hanged Gordon Cummins, the so-called 'Blackout

Ripper'. The governor of Norwich prison puts forward the name of Pierrepoint's assistant, a Grimsby man named Harry Kirk. Kirk's name appears on the approved list of executioners and he has assisted before at Norwich executions, but so far has never led one. Both executioners know the routine. It starts with them entering the prison the night before, under cover of darkness, out of sight of the inmates. They will then need to lodge inside the prison, close to the place of execution. This is usually a room above the condemned prisoner's cell. On the day of execution, they will visit Wyeth in his cell, with prison guards on standby, to bind Wyeth's hands together with a leather strap. They will then escort him from his cell toward the gallows, just a short walk down the corridor, and guide him up onto the platform. A hood will then be placed over Wyeth's head, closely followed by the noose around his neck. The noose will be tightened and checked once more. Seconds later, Pierrepoint will step to one side and pull the lever to open the trap door beneath Wyeth and send him to oblivion. This will be seen as a just punishment for Wyeth taking the life of an innocent child.

With Wyeth's execution planned for just over two weeks' time, the prison governor is making sure everything is in place for it to run smoothly. The nation has seen the police investigation and subsequent trial splashed across all the newspapers, so there will no doubt be heightened interest on the day of execution. The governor knows a botched execution will put him under that spotlight, reflecting badly upon how he is running the prison. Another formality, usual when the death penalty is declared, is for the Secretary of State to be informed.

MONDAY, 20TH JULY, 1942

Syndicated news reports – *An appeal is to be lodged on behalf of Private James Wyeth (22), Pioneer Corps, who is under sentence of death for the murder of Patricia Ann Cupit (6), a London evacuee. guilty of murder and sentenced to death.*

Chief Inspector Thomas Barratt has consistently displayed impartiality with his investigation, and subsequent conviction, of James Wyeth. Today, he writes to the Superintendent of Norfolk County Constabulary to outline how he felt the trial went. As expected, his letter does not strike a triumphant tone at Wyeth's conviction. Instead, one observation he does make, is he felt the defence seemed happy to accept the prosecution's assertion their client did in fact attack Pat, not once testing that claim. Barratt also refers to the fact the defence only called two witnesses – a doctor, and Wyeth's mother.

The main reason for Barratt's letter is to pass on his

grateful thanks for the assistance lent to him by the police of Norfolk County Constabulary. He singles out Detective Inspectors Garner and Dye, Detective Constables Barker and Dingle, and Detective Sergeant Webb.

TUESDAY, 21ST JULY, 1942

The congratulations continue, when Stephen Van Neck, Chief Constable of Norfolk County Constabulary writes to New Scotland Yard praising the work ethic of Chief Inspector Barratt and Detective Sergeant Webb.

"Chief Inspector Barratt and Sergeant Webb turned out to be the type of Police Officer who understood how to work in very happy co-operation with the Officers of my Force. They were sound and methodical, and keen to clear up the case. I should be glad, provided you agree, if this commendation could be recorded in the official history sheet of the two Detective Officers concerned."

New Scotland Yard, when replying to Van Neck, cast doubt upon Wyeth's sentence.

"… it is quite certain we shall need a summary of evidence and statements which bear on the state of the murderer's mind. Home Office are bound to be pressed to go into the question of insanity, but first I gather there is to be the Court of Criminal Appeal."

Notwithstanding the probable appeal, Norwich prison

staff must continue their preparations to carry out the sentence. The High Sherriff of Norfolk, is informed Wyeth's planned execution date has been put back two days and will now take place at 8am, on Thursday 6th August.

In light of the Home Office taking a keen interest in Wyeth's trial, and subsequently the medical officer at Norwich prison being ordered to personally assess the condemned man's mental state, the past forty-eight hours has seen constant updates on the prisoner. The Governor of Norwich prison, upon receiving these, has been updating the Prison Commission, with the latter now informing a conference of prison governors hosted within the Home Office. Further along the chain of command, two of the country's most senior civil servants are also informed - William Henry Waddams, of the Police Commission, and Sir Frank Aubrey, in the Home Office. The two men discuss escalating the matter to involve a statutory inquiry into Wyeth's mental condition, meaning the inquiry is fully backed by the law, with those involved subject to consequences if they do not comply.

WEDNESDAY, 22ND JULY, 1942

Formal documentation is received by the Registrar of the Criminal Court of Appeal, that Wyeth is to appeal his conviction.

"I, the above-named Appellant, hereby give you notice that I desire to appeal to the Court of Criminal Appeal against my conviction and sentence on the grounds hereinafter set forth on page 2 of this notice."

The document is a standard Home Office form, with Wyeth's details typed out. It indicates he has not filed this himself, but instead been instructed by his solicitor, Greenland Houchan & Co, of Norwich, probably during a visit by them, to him, at Norwich prison. Wyeth who claimed legal aid for costs at his trial, now requests the same for his appeal. The document does not state the reason for the appeal, but instead reserves the right to reveal that later. It also reserves Wyeth's right to attend the appeal hearing if he so wishes. It is not known if the defence has found more expert witnesses, as Chief Inspector Barratt pointed out they only called two for the trial, but it at least buys them time.

Although Chief Inspector Barratt's involvement is over, and he is now working on other cases, he still finds time to formally write a confidential report to the Commanding Officer of Britain's Home Forces, General Bernard Paget. Barratt updates Paget about the trial and subsequent outcome, perhaps in response to Paget's request for information about why one of his soldiers is facing execution. The trial has now reached into the upper echelons of the government and the British military.

THURSDAY, 23ᴿᴰ JULY, 1942

Attention to James Wyeth's death sentence is growing. So is the pressure to assess the prisoner's mental condition. The National Scheme for Disabled Men writes to Norwich prison, demanding Wyeth is classed as, "not mentally normal".

The charity goes on to suggest Wyeth therefore cannot be held, "altogether responsible for his actions".

The Secretary of State, Percy Grigg, requests that once the upcoming appeal has concluded, then all documentation on the case should be passed directly to him, so he can personally review the matter.

FRIDAY, 24ᵀᴴ JULY, 1942

The formal reasons for the appeal against Wyeth's sentence are given by his defence. They believe the evidence provided in court should have led the jury to convict Wyeth as guilty but insane. They also believe that Justice Wrottesley misdirected the jury in his summing up, by not referring to their medical evidence stating Wyeth was insane. In particular, the appeal makes reference to the judge's statement, whereby he intimates someone with a mental condition can choose, if they so wish to do so, to control their condition.

"… *that impulses to which human nature is liable may include terrible, beastly, cruel impulses and that it was the duty of all of us to resist evil impulses and that the fact that a person does not resist a wrong impulse is not insanity or the Criminal Courts of this country might go out of work.*"

The defence also point out the fact that little weight was given to the fact Wyeth's aunt and sister are detained in institutions for poor mental health, which they believe, indicate a family predisposed to being "abnormal".

MONDAY, 27TH JULY, 1942

A mental health organisation, the Central Association for Mental Welfare, lobby the Assistant Director of Public Prosecutions, Arthur Sefton Cohen, to review Wyeth's mental health. The Home Office declares it will indeed conduct a statutory inquiry into Wyeth's mental condition whatever the outcome of his appeal.

FRIDAY, 31ST JULY, 1942

A piece of paper is passed to the Governor of Norwich prison. He can see it has travelled through the official channels, but is nothing like the usual prison documentation usually given to him. Someone has handwritten, in light blue ink, on a blank piece of paper. It is dated from three days ago, sent from a post office in Wales, but has ended up on the desk of the Governor. He reads it.

"c/o Blaenwaun Post Office, Whitland 28.7.42

Dear Sir.

Re. Pte James Wyeth

Convicted for murder of a young girl. 2 or 3 weeks ago.

I shall be very thankful to you if you will hand this enclosed letter to my son. I do not know in what prison he is. Thanking you.

Kate Crane."

The letter claims it has been written by Wyeth's natural mother, Kate Crane, who has shown no interest in his life until now. Perhaps his notoriety, his name printed in newspapers across the nation, has finally reached her? She has been known to travel the land, so chances are the news has only just reached her. The letter, in two parts, could be from anyone, so the Governor orders an investigation into its origin.

MONDAY, 10ᵀᴴ AUGUST, 1942

The Carmarthenshire police confirm to Norwich prison the letter has been sent by Wyeth's natural mother, as stated, from the post office in Blaenwaun. The prison authorities finally hand the letter to Wyeth. What Wyeth does with the letter, no one knows. It will be lost in the time after he receives it. Was the text in the letter a final act from Kate Crane distancing herself from her son? Perhaps even admonishing him? Or did she finally show him the love he had lacked since birth?

WEDNESDAY, 12TH AUGUST, 1942

The date of Wyeth's appeal is finally confirmed as being 25th August. As always, Chief Inspector Barratt maintains an interest and informs the Chief Constable of Norfolk County Constabulary, Stephen Van Neck, just in case he was not aware.

TUESDAY, 18TH AUGUST, 1942

During Wyeth's time in Brixton, before his trial, while his mental state was being assessed, he received correspondence from a woman trying to direct him along the path of religion. At the conclusion of the trial, she wrote to him again, but wrongly assumed he was still being held there. The prison returned her letters as "not known", but she persisted and wrote to the prison service enquiring about his whereabouts. Her letter finally arrives at Norwich prison.

She introduces herself as S.B. Meadows, and admits she is not related or known to Wyeth. Accompanying her letter is an evangelical booklet titled, 'Why Doesn't God Intervene?', which aims to explain why there is so much death and misery in the world and, as it quotes, "man's inhumanity to man".

Containing fourteen pages of why God will allow the war to carry on uninterrupted unless men repent their sins, the prison officers wonder its relevance to Wyeth, or even if he has the capacity to read and understand it. However, this is not the first, nor will it be the last, unsolicited correspondence to Wyeth. There is widespread interest in saving Wyeth's soul. Such correspondence is not passed on to Wyeth. Indeed, in this instance Norwich prison writes back to Meadows, thanking her for her letter and informing her that the prison already provides religious reading material for those inmates who wish to read them.

WYETH'S APPEAL

James Wyeth appears at the Court of Criminal Appeal wearing his khaki woollen battledress. Despite his murder conviction, he has not yet been formally discharged from the army, so is still entitled to wear his British Army uniform. He stands before the three Appeal judges – Justices Humphreys, Hilbery and Tucker; along with his defence barrister, Frank Alpe. Also in the courtroom is the prosecution barrister, Sir Charles Doughty.

This is not a re-trial, so there will be no drawn-out witness examinations, and in fact Wyeth is one of twenty appeals to be heard, although some will have to run into tomorrow. The defence will be given just enough time to outline their case, and the prosecution the same to counter the defence argument. The three judges will then confer, with Humphreys having the final say about the validity of Justice Wrottesley's sentence. Why Wyeth is there is unclear, he took virtually no part in the trial and is unlikely to be called to the witness stand today, however it is proper that he hears the verdict of the Appeal Court. Also brought to the hearing is the forensic evidence of Pat and Wyeth's clothing, just in case it is referred to, although this bears absolutely no relevance to the defence's claim that Wyeth was insane when he attacked Pat. Wyeth is not the only man to be pleading for his life today. Three others are to appear after Wyeth, all fighting against their respective death penalties.

Frank Alpe outlines his case. He suggests the question of insanity was not put clearly to the jury. He also claims in Wyeth's trial, the judge failed to tell the jury about Wyeth's family history of mental illness. He tells the Appeal judges that if Wrottesley had done so, then the jury would have added more weight to the testimony of Dr Louis Rose, who spoke of Wyeth suffering hysterical automatism. Alpe tells the three judges:

"My case is that Wyeth has been abnormal all his life and subject to black-outs in which he committed offences."

Justice Humphreys, speaking on behalf of the three judges, replies that Wyeth brutally attacked Pat, but then attempted to cover her lifeless body, which he believes is not the action of someone not knowing what they had done was wrong. He suggests, if the prisoner had blacked out when attacking her, then he would surely have just left her lying there. Humphreys goes on to say that Wyeth made two statements to the police, one denying knowing anything about the attack, and the other admitting to it, which did not demonstrate Wyeth knew nothing of the attack. In fact by the time he gave the second statement he recalled every moment and even took the police to the crime scene, commentating throughout about what he had done. Humphreys does acknowledge there was evidence presented at the trial that might indicate Wyeth acted under an uncontrollable impulse, but, as Justice Wrottesley pointed out, this in itself cannot be accepted as evidence of insanity. Humphreys also declares that the trial judge's summing up was full and fair, so he finds no misdirection in it. Without even requiring input from the prosecution, Humphreys ends proceedings and dismisses the defence's appeal. Almost as quick as it started, it is over. Wyeth is not spared.

The relevant authorities are then informed by communique, including Norwich prison, who will now proceed with arrangements for the execution.

"In the High Court of Criminal Appeal, Criminal Appeal Act, 1907. Notification of result of application to the full court, Rex vs James Wyeth.

To the Prison Commissioners of His Majesty's Prison at Norwich.

THIS IS TO GIVE YOU NOTICE that the Court of Criminal Appeal, as duly constituted for the hearing of Appeals under the Act, has this day considered the Application of the above-named Appellant for leave to appeal against conviction and has determined the same, and has refused the said application.

Dated this 25th day of August A.D.1942.

Carrol Romer, Registrar of the Court of Criminal Appeal."

Leicester Evening Mail – *Condemned soldier appeals in vain.*

Manchester Evening News – *Soldier loses his case.*

Gloucestershire Echo – *Death sentence upheld.*

SATURDAY, 29TH AUGUST, 1942

In light of Wyeth's appeal being dismissed, the High Sherriff for Norfolk confirms a new date for the execution to take place. It is now destined for 8am, Thursday 10th September, 1942. Harry Kirk, who up to now has only ever assisted at executions, is now named as the principal executioner. The authorities' search for his assistant is a short one, and the name of Stephen Wade is put forward for the position.

TUESDAY 1ST SEPTEMBER, 1942

The Home Office, having considered the rejection of Wyeth's appeal, now issue a communication to the Prison Commission.

"I am directed by the Secretary of State to inform you that he

has decided to direct a Medical Inquiry under Section 2 (4) of the Criminal Lunatics Act, 1884, to be held into the mental condition of James Wyeth, who is now lying under sentence of death in His Majesty's Prison at Norwich, and that he has requested Dr W.N. East, formerly Medical Commissioner of His Majesty's Prison, and Dr J.S. Hopwood, Medical Superintendent of Broadmoor Criminal Lunatic Asylum, to conduct the same.

I am, Sir, Your obedient Servant, Frank Aubrey Newsome."

Frank Newsome is Deputy Under-Secretary of State, and as such there is probably no more senior civil servant within the Home Office. Ironically, he is known to be a supporter of capital punishment, but in this instance, he has ordered an inquiry into Wyeth's mental state.

WEDNESDAY, 2ND SEPTEMBER, 1942

Dr East and Dr Hopwood waste no time in visiting Norwich prison. The Governor of the prison writes in his journal that both visited Wyeth today. Dr Hopwood's inclusion is most interesting because he has vast experience of assessing inmates held at Broadmoor secure hospital. It now seems Wyeth's future could be destined to be decided by what these two doctors report back.

A communique is issued from the Home Office, Whitehall, London, SW1.

"*Sir,*

I am directed by the Secretary of State to inform you that he has had under his consideration the case of James Wyeth, now in the prison at Norwich, having been sentenced to death, and that he has advised His Majesty to respite the capital sentence with a view to the immediate removal of the prisoner to Broadmoor Criminal Lunatic Asylum. The prisoner has been certified to be insane under Section 2 (4) of the Criminal Lunatics Act, 1884.

I am, Sir, Your obedient servant, A Maxwell"

It is worth noting the relevant section from the Act, states the following:

"*In the case of a prisoner under sentence of death, if it appears to a Secretary of State, either by means of a certificate signed by two members of the visiting committee of the prison in which such prisoner is confined, or by any other means, that there is reason to believe such prisoner to be insane, the Secretary of State shall appoint two or more legally qualified medical practitioners, and the said medical practitioners shall forthwith examine such prisoner and inquire as to his insanity, and after such examination and inquiry such practitioners shall make a report in writing to the Secretary of State as to the sanity of the prisoner, and they, or the majority of them, may certify in writing that he is insane."*

Those outside the Home Office may not have known at the time, but this section refers to events that began a month before the appeal even took place. The meeting of two civil servants, William Waddams and Sir Frank Aubrey, in which they concluded Wyeth to likely be insane, should have triggered the request for two medical practitioners to examine the prisoner further, and report to the Secretary of State. However, the Home Office waited to see how the appeal played out. Following the hearing, two doctors, Dr East and Dr Hopwood, were then instructed to conduct their examinations, independent of each other. The doctors' findings, having been reported to the Home Office, have now rendered that appeal process irrelevant. The highest court in the land has been overruled.

With this ruling, James Wyeth is spared the hangman's noose, although it has taken no small effort on behalf of top civil servants in the Home Office, prison governors, doctors and ultimately informing the King, to arrange this. We must also remember the mental health charities that took an interest, and not forgetting those of a religious disposition who wanted to save Wyeth's soul. It seems the will of the people was not always that Wyeth should pay the ultimate price for slaying an innocent child. The governor of Norwich prison immediately acknowledges receipt of the Home Office communique. In his reply, he notes that Stephen Wade had accepted the invitation to assist with the execution, but has since been informed his services are no longer required. Plans will now be made for the removal of Wyeth and his transfer to Broadmoor. The medical officer at Norwich prison fills in Wyeth's medical papers.

"Form of insanity: Polymorphism (Primary dementia)

When the symptoms appeared: Unknown

Opinion as to the patient's state of mind and degree of responsibility, at the time when offence was committed: Unsound mind and not aware of his actions.

Having been previously insane: No"

If Pat's family are rueing this decision, especially considering her father's demand for vengeance in the early days of the investigation, then the feeling of elation felt by Evelyn Wyeth, James's adopted mother, is the polar opposite. Not only has the life of her son been saved, but with him being moved from Norwich to Broadmoor the distance she will have to travel from her home to visit him, is no longer 150 miles, but instead 16 miles.

TUESDAY, 8TH SEPTEMBER, 1942

James Wyeth is removed from Norwich prison and

transferred to Broadmoor. His transfer is made very low key, in fact there is a delay in alerting the media.

THURSDAY, 10TH SEPTEMBER, 1942

Daily Mail – *Murderer not to die.*

Birmingham Daily Gazette – *Condemned man insane.*

Shields Daily News – *Girl murderer is certified insane. Private James Wyeth (22) of the Pioneer Corps, sentenced to death at the Old Bailey in July for the murder of Patricia Ann Cupit, six-year-old London evacuee, has been certified insane and the Home Secretary has ordered his removal to Broadmoor.*

Now that Wyeth is to spend his days in Broadmoor and there will be no execution to report on, today's headlines - albeit delayed after Wyeth's official transfer from Norwich - will be the last in relation to Wyeth, or Pat and her murder on Riddlesworth Park. Over the past four months the newspapers have kept their readers updated on key moments in the case. Initially, the story kept Pat's name in people's thoughts. Then, with the apprehension of her attacker, it was Wyeth's name that was the main focus. Yet, after today, their names will disappear and the story will ultimately be largely forgotten.

The Norwich prison governor receives a circular, sent by the Prison Commission to all prison governors, which he instantly recognises as referring to James Wyeth's trial.

"A case having occurred recently, in which a prisoner, while awaiting trial, was specially examined by means of an electro-encephalogram, the Commissioners think that medical officers may be interested in the following report upon the present state of electro-encephalography. This minute should, therefore, be handed to the medical officer of your establishment for his information and retention.

G.J. RONS, Chief Clerk, Prison Commission."

The circular refers to a research paper on the electro-encephalogram (E.E.G.), the machine the Home Secretary, Herbert Morrison, sent Wyeth to be tested on. Morrison must have given some weight to the validity of the machine, otherwise he would not have stepped in to send Wyeth to be tested. The result of that test was then produced by the defence as evidence of insanity at the trial. This paper, released on 26th July, which was after Wyeth's trial but ahead of his appeal, raises some interesting points over the validity of the E.E.G. as a tool to diagnose someone as being insane.

The paper acknowledges the equipment, which has only been in operation for seven years in Britain and is not yet widely available, can confirm the presence of epilepsy, brain tumours and physical brain trauma, however the equipment is yet to diagnose mental disorders or chemical imbalances in the brain. Of those who were tested and known to have epilepsy before taking the test, 60 per cent were picked up by the equipment, the rest showed a normal result. This means the equipment can only be used to support a diagnosis, it cannot alone be used to find epilepsy. In the United States, the equipment picked up abnormalities in one out of every ten people tested, although it didn't necessarily mean they had epilepsy. However, of those, many did in fact have relatives who have epilepsy, so perhaps it can pick up traits of the illness in those who are not showing outward symptoms. Wyeth may well have qualified as being in the 10 per cent, on account of his sister being institutionalised through epilepsy. The paper also reports of this group, a significant number had "… *abnormal personalities, particularly those with violent, aggressive and impulsive traits.*"

It continued:

"*This has been established both in children and adults, and it is therefore probable that a percentage of individuals convicted of crime of violence will show non-specific abnormalities in the EEG. These would not indicate that such criminals were necessarily epileptic, but only that they were pre-disposed to a group of disorders of which epilepsy and psychopathic personality are the commonest.*

Since the E.E.G. can only show certain electrical functions of the brain cells which as far as is known at present are only modifiable by chemical and physical changes in the brain, the test cannot indicate what is or what has been in a person's mind at any time. It can give no indication of a person's sanity or insanity. Even if the test proves that the individual tested is epileptic, it cannot alone produce evidence of past automatism, or of a person's thoughts, awareness or intentions at any time in the past."

The paper, using James Wyeth as a case study, invalidates the test as proof of someone's insanity, or of an accused's mental state when they carried out an act that they are later brought to account for. Had the paper been released before Wyeth's trial, then the defence may have been less confident bringing it as evidence, leaving them with just Wyeth's mother and one doctor's assessment to their meagre presentation. In fact, this paper backs the judge's decision to not pay much attention to it. The paper will also certainly limit the value of the E.E.G. when brought to future courtrooms.

TUESDAY, 15TH SEPTEMBER, 1942

Perhaps as a consequence of James Wyeth's trial, William Waddams, of the Police Commission, sends a memo to all prison governors. It covers the subject of servicemen, detained in civilian prisons following a court martial, and who might be classified as being a "mental defective". It seems, at the very least, the Wyeth trial may have brought prisoners' mental health to the fore. Waddams instructs the prison governors that the Mental Deficiency Act covers those serving in the Armed Forces, not just civilians, which means more servicemen could be heading for institutions like Broadmoor.

WEDNESDAY, 16TH SEPTEMBER, 1942

The Commissioner of the Metropolitan Police commends the two detectives from New Scotland Yard for their speedy conclusion of this murder case. Chief Inspector Thomas Barratt is "highly commended" for his "determination and adroitness in a difficult case of murder." While Detective Sergeant Albert Webb is "commended" for "valuable assistance in a difficult case of murder."

The citation also records the following:

"This case was brought to a successful issue by speedy, thorough, and skilful investigation. The Chief Inspector was faced with a difficult task owing to there being soldiers

stationed in the vicinity of the crime. Hundreds of them were interviewed, and by process of elimination the Corporal in charge of a small squad, of which Wyeth was a unit, was seen. In result of that interview Wyeth was interrogated but denied any knowledge of the murder. Then followed a careful interrogation of other members of the squad, when it was found that Wyeth's statement contained many inaccuracies. Further interrogation of the suspect drove him into a corner. When realising his position hopeless, he made a full confession. In the meantime, his clothing had been microscopically examined and revealed human bloodstains and fibres of the dress worn by the murdered child."

MONDAY, 19TH OCTOBER, 1942

Patricia Ann Cupit should have been spoiled and made to feel very loved today. But then, in her parents' eyes, she has always been special to them, their only child. Yet, even though her parents wrote and visited when they could, they would have made an extra effort to be with her on this day. A sumptuous tea would have been laid on at the Pasks' home, where there would have been cake, perhaps candles, and most definitely a present or two. Today, Little Pat should have excitedly celebrated her seventh birthday. Her seventh birthday denied to her by someone who acted in a moment of madness. A maniacal rage, as it were. She should have been sat at the Pasks' table, blowing out those birthday cake candles, momentarily making a wish, then smiling gleefully as she looked up, surrounded by friends and family who loved her dearly. Instead, the only way her parents could show her love on that birthday was the placing of flowers upon her grave.

PART FIVE – POSTSCRIPT

THE MURDERER

James Wyeth was fortunate to have avoided the death sentence. During the war, at a time when the focus was on killing the enemy and preventing them from invading, there were few resources to investigate mental disorders. On the surface, it may have seemed less effort to hang him, than to try to understand his issues and to address them. However, in 1942, as subsequently seen in the aftermath of Wyeth's trial, and despite the depravities of war, there saw the beginnings of a change in attitudes to mental health. In November of that year, Sir William Beveridge released his report, entitled, '*Social Insurance and Allied Services*'. It would pave the way for the introduction of the National Health Service six years later, a social service that would be inclusive for all, including people like Wyeth. Its introduction opened up exciting new avenues for assessment and treatment of mental health issues.

During the 1950s, while Wyeth was being held in Broadmoor, outliving most of those who had overseen his trial, there began a groundswell of public concern about the treatment of people with mental illness. This groundswell resulted in the Mental Health Act being brought into law. One key aspect of the new act saw a move from holding 'inmates' in large psychiatric hospitals, and instead integrating people with mental health issues into community-based services. *The Percy Commission*, of 1957, which contributed to the act, stated the following:

"It is now generally considered, in the best interests of the patients who are fit to live in the community, that they should not be in large mental institutions such as the present mental and mental deficiency hospitals. Nor is it the proper function of the hospital authority to provide residential accommodation for patients who do not require hospital or specialist services."

In truth, Wyeth was probably not aware of the Mental Health Act, nor what implications, if any, it might mean for him, although he did later benefit from it.

Pat's killer eventually died on 3rd October 1983, with the cause of death stated on his death certificate as, "Myocardial infarction, coronary occlusion". A heart attack. His death certificate includes both his natural and his adopted surnames – *James Crane Edward Thomas Wyeth*; and was signed on behalf of the Royal Surrey Hospital, Guildford, on account of no next of kin being available at the time. Importantly, the hospital is a public one, not a prison hospital. His death certificate does not list Broadmoor, but instead a home address for him, as being, "*Brunswick Lodge, Argyle Street, Reading*". In 1983, this building was a 'halfway house' for integrating people recovering from mental illness. Therefore, by the time of his death, Wyeth had become a beneficiary of the Mental Health Act and had been discharged from Broadmoor to secure a place in society. So far, I have not been able to ascertain the exact date of his discharge, the archive relating to his release is held at the Royal Berkshire Archives, with access restricted to Wyeth's immediate family for one hundred years from his death. Nonetheless, the Broadmoor medical officers must have assessed him as no longer suffering a mental disorder, nor prone to sudden outbursts of violence, thus he was safe to be integrated into society. A prognosis that would have made his adopted mother stand tall with pride.

Whatever our thoughts are of James Wyeth, there can be no excuse for his act of violence upon a defenceless child. However, he was clearly a troubled soul from birth, with professionals suggesting varying therapies from strict regimes to counselling, to others that were overlooked by the courts. Despite the regimes of borstal, the army and prison, his problems looked incurable. When his peers came to a crossroads, to either end his life or rehabilitate, they eventually chose the latter. At that time, in 1942, even the most optimistic may have had doubts about his prognosis. Yet, in the aftermath of war, the nation came together, not to specifically save

Wyeth, but to create an inclusive nation, one that he ultimately benefitted from. He very much should have felt fortunate to be alive.

WYETH'S ADOPTED MOTHER

Evelyn Gladys Wyeth remained at her family home in Cedars Road, Maidenhead, with her husband, undeterred by the national publicity generated by her son's arrest and subsequent trial. It is worth noting her address was often reported in full in the newspapers during that time, something Wyeth's natural mother did not have to endure, nor anyone else for that matter. This is the price Evelyn paid for her love of her adopted son. Evelyn died ten years after her son's conviction for murder, when she was aged just 54. It is not known if the stress of the trial contributed to Evelyn's early demise, but she did at least experience the joy of her natural son, Derrick, getting married a few months before she passed away. She had treated Wyeth, throughout his life, as her own flesh and blood too.

THE NATURAL MOTHER

There is some evidence that Wyeth's natural mother, Kathleen (Kate) Cordelia Crane, left behind her travelling lifestyle after her son was convicted, and reconnected with her daughter Olive. Olive left the institution she had been housed in for many years and went on to lead a normal life, perhaps as a result of her epilepsy being better controlled. Olive married and raised a large family, meaning her life story is one of triumph over adversity. At some point, Kate was photographed proudly standing in the doorway of Olive's house with one of Olive's daughters – Kate's granddaughter; although Kate's contact with her daughter was fleeting and not sustained. Kate outlived her older siblings, and died in 1968, aged 68. It is not currently known if she reconnected with her estranged son while he was in prison, or even if her extended family are aware of him.

THE VICTIM'S EVACUEE PARENTS

Albert Robert Pask and Florence Melinda Baker married in October 1937, moving to Riddlesworth that same year. They remained together until Albert's death in September 1985. According to his obituary in a local newspaper, he and his wife lived in Riddlesworth for forty-eight years, until moving seven miles down the road, to the village of Hepworth, Albert's birthplace, six months before he died. It transpires Albert was a Great War hero, having gone to fight in the trenches of Flanders with the Suffolk Regiment in August 1915, then being wounded on more than one occasion. The obituary states his funeral was attended by a "*Mr A Balls*", perhaps the lad Albert Balls, who was with Mr Pask when they discovered Pat lying under the tree. If so, it provides proof they remained close family friends for more than four decades. Albert Pask died aged 74 years old. His widow, Flo died in January 2008, aged 92.

THE VICTIM'S NATURAL PARENTS

Pat's parents, Leonard Claude Cupit and Anne Julia Cupit, had another daughter in 1946, who they named Susan. After the war, the couple ran a hotel, the Crown and Anchor Hotel, on Portsmouth Road, Esher, London, but both continued to struggle with the loss of their 'Little Pat'. It was said that Anne, would often be found in her nightdress at the side of her daughter's grave. In 1951 the couple split up. Leonard initially moved to the Berystede Hotel, to carry on with his catering career. He later remarried and died in November 2001, aged 88. Anne moved to Long Ditton, London, and following the divorce, returned to using her maiden name of Boyle, until remarrying in 1966. She died in October 1981. It transpires Anne had fallen pregnant in 1931, years before meeting Leonard, and had given birth to a girl. The child remained with the baby's father when the couple split and Anne never saw her again, which probably had a lasting effect. That daughter, the older half-sister of Pat and Susan, had also been given the name of Patricia Anne.

THE JUDGE

The Right Honourable Sir Frederic John Wrottesley first qualified in law in 1907, and his forty years career was only interrupted by the Great War, when he went to France as a Major in the Royal Field Artillery. In 1947, he received a peerage and was appointed to the Privy Council. The following year, in October 1948, he was forced to retire due to his failing health. He died a month later, at his home, aged 68.

THE PROSECUTION

Before the war, Sir Charles Doughty was renowned for being a fair arbitrator of trade disputes. This led to him being knighted by the Government in 1941 for services to the Ministry of Labour and National Service. He died at his London home in May 1956, aged 77. At the time of his death, one of his sons, also named Charles, was Member of Parliament for East Surrey.

THE DEFENCE.

Frank Theodore Alpe continued practising law, splitting his life between Wymondham and London. He died on

25th January 1952, at the Norfolk and Norwich Hospital, aged 66. Despite being a lawyer, he died intestate, meaning he left no will. Fortunately for his widow, she was still his only beneficiary.

THE DETECTIVE

Chief Inspector Thomas Barratt joined the Metropolitan Police in 1920, initially serving as a Police Constable. Due to his thorough investigations and dedication, he was not a constable long, instead successive promotions saw him rise through the ranks quickly. Within a few years he had become a detective within New Scotland Yard and, upon reaching the rank of Chief Inspector, was the force's go-to detective to head up investigations, especially murders. In January 1943, West Sussex police were investigating the murder of a servicewoman, who in circumstances similar to Patricia Cupit, had been left dying on a lonely road. They requested assistance from New Scotland Yard and without hesitation, Barratt was the man they sent. He was promoted to Chief Superintendent in 1949 and went on to lead some of the highest profile investigations in Britian – Neville Heath, the 'Lady Killer' (1946), John Haigh, the 'acid bath murderer' (1949), the theft of the Coronation Stone from Westminster Abbey (1950), the £250,000 mailbag robbery (1952), and the arrest of John Christie who had strangled seven women in Notting Hill (1953). It led the Sunday Mirror to label Barratt as, "the Yard's famous murder chief".

During his career, Barratt received twenty-four

commendations for his police work and was awarded the M.B.E. in 1952. By the mid-1950s he was heading up the Metropolitan Police Detective Training School at Hendon. In late 1956, he was in Westminster Hospital recovering from a serious operation, when he recognised a patient who he knew to be a convicted trickster. Barratt, always alert, observed the man asking for money from other patients. The detective, although himself being a patient at the time, still tipped off his colleagues, who promptly arrested the man once he was discharged from hospital. Barratt was through-and-through a policeman, even when seriously ill in hospital. However, it would be his last-ever case. He died in March 1957, at the same hospital, just a week from his planned retirement and his sixtieth birthday.

PATRICIA ANN CUPIT

Patricia Ann Cupit will always be regarded as Wyeth's last victim. Yet, she deserves more than that, so I shall give her the last word in this story. Her passing, at such an early age, means that outside the circumstances of her death there is nothing much else to say about her life. So, with that in mind, what happened after she died?

I know in life Pat was happy, she loved her parents and she enjoyed staying with Mr and Mrs Pask in Riddlesworth. Some say she was mature for her age, she definitely thought she was, as she mentioned in her last letter to her father:

"I am a big girl now, I can read, skip, knit and tell the time. Do you like my real handwriting?"

Pat's body was interred at Streatham Park Cemetery, London, in plot number 36505. During the funeral, her grave was adorned with many floral tributes. A headstone was erected shortly after, but in the four decades that followed, the headstone became unsafe. In 1986, the cemetery deemed it unsafe and liable to fall over, perhaps injuring a visitor, so they wrote to Pat's parents requesting it be made safe. Sadly, her mother had passed away by that time, and her father was not living at the wartime address held by the cemetery. The cemetery's request went unanswered. Pat's headstone was removed, along with many others around her grave, and for almost forty years she laid in an unmarked grave among other unmarked graves, making it virtually impossible to identify the exact location of her grave. Even the grave markers were gone and it looked as though few people ever visited that part of the cemetery. I was never able to locate exactly where she lay when I visited, so I always estimated and laid flowers in the vicinity. That might have been all I could tell you about Pat's grave, had events not taken a turn recently.

Back in 2010, I was contacted by Susan Cupit, Pat's younger sister, after she had seen some notes I put on the internet about Pat's murder. It seems Susan's parents had told her very little about her sister's death, so she enquired about what other information I had. In return she supplied Pat's photo that features in this book and we corresponded briefly. Also, over the years, I have kept in touch with Susan's daughter, Anna, who is Pat's niece. When Susan passed away in 2022, the ownership of Pat's plot was passed to Anna. She, dismayed that Pat had no headstone, put plans together to correct that and, in May 2024, a headstone was installed to serve as a proper memorial to Pat. The inscription reads:

"*Angel wings, upon the clouds,*

Your body softly sleeps,

Hush now little princess,

No more tears you have to keep."

Below the text, an image of a teddy bear features, which appears to hold a book:

"Little Pat. Forever in our hearts".

At this point I would like to thank Delphine Evon, a resident of Streatham, London. Upon hearing of Pat's headstone being installed she made a beeline to the cemetery to find it. This was a trip she had made twice before in anticipation of seeing the new headstone, only to find it not yet in place, meaning she was unable to locate Pat's grave. During a video call to me, where I assisted her locate the headstone, Delphine excitedly announced she had found it, then placed flowers and spent time by Pat's graveside. I feel this demonstrates how Pat's story has brought people together, who were previously unknown to each other. A story with Pat placed firmly in people's hearts.

Over the years, I have released snippets of my research locally, which has generated some support for a plaque or memorial to remember Pat, somewhere near or on Riddlesworth Park. It is worth noting the army camp that Wyeth was billeted at was given over to Polish families after the war, and a memorial has been erected nearby to remember them. So, a precedent has been set. It is still early days yet, but with the publication of this book, there will hopefully be renewed interest in such a commemorative feature for her. A feature that will spark an interest in a little girl's life that was so cruelly taken. At the very least, I hope that in you, the reader of this book, Pat's memory will live on and she is no longer forgotten.

PART SIX - PAT'S STORY & ME

This part is not central to Pat's story, but you may be interested in how I eventually came to write the book. I never went looking for Pat, instead she found me.

It began more than twenty years ago, before archived information could be readily found on the internet. I would travel to my local Records Office in Bury St. Edmunds, searching for wartime references of my hometown of Brandon, Suffolk. While sat in front of a microfilm machine, scrolling through scanned copies of local newspapers, then making notes in a pad, I found something of interest in a 1942 edition of the *Bury Free Press*. A title read, '*Riddlesworth Park Murder*', standing out between stories of lesser crimes, such as a man accused of stealing pheasant eggs and another of stealing RAF furniture. The park is just minutes from where I live, so I read the report, which offered nothing but a distraction from the focus of my research. I didn't even make any notes. During the following week's visit, I read about a soldier confessing to the murder. Intrigued, I scrolled back through earlier editions and caught up with reports that had not previously caught my attention. It was now I began making notes. Anyone who has undertaken research will tell you, you often find something of interest and make a note. It may lead to nothing and remain on the unturned pages of a notepad, but occasionally another piece of the jigsaw falls into place.

Subsequent visits to the Records Office slowly unravelled the extent of the huge story. Yet, at the time, there was seemingly nothing other than the newspaper reports about it, it was certainly the case that no one locally had heard of it. I created a basic website to share my research, of which, one page included a few notes on Pat's murder. In 2010, I received an email, from someone who had seen that webpage, and it would change forever my outlook on Pat's story. The email was sent by Susan Cupit, who introduced herself as Pat's younger sister. It seems Susan's mother never talked much about what happened to Pat, so Susan learned much of her sister's fate when she discovered my website. In return, Susan offered to send me a photograph of Pat. I am not given to showing emotion very easily, but when I saw Pat for the first time, the child I had only known by name, it reduced me to tears. In 2010, that child should have grown to be my grandmother's age, but instead, for eternity, she will remain a child. That moment ignited a journey.

In May, 2019, me and my wife, who were staying in London for a weekend break, made, what was for me, an emotional first time visit to find Pat's grave. We caught various Tube trains and buses, not really sure of where we were going, and ended up at Streatham Park Cemetery. We had Pat's plot number, so were confident we would find her. However, we were met with a large area of long grass minus any headstones. I laid flowers and a photo of Pat at a spot I estimated her resting place to be. When we returned home, I filed a Freedom of Information request to The National Archives, to open a closed file – PCOM 9/705. The file related to James Wyeth being found guilty but declared insane. I had been aware of it for a few months, but was not sure, nor confident, of the process to request access to it. My initial request was turned down, but upon appeal, the file, in its redacted form, was released into the public domain. Any intention to view the file was curtailed by the lockdown of 2020, although the following year I did get to see it. Tucked away in that file was a mugshot from when Wyeth was sent to borstal. It was the first time I saw Wyeth's face, the face of the man who killed Pat. I was shocked at how normal he looked. I was expecting, perhaps hoping, to see the face of evil. I wondered about his story.

Those initial research days at Bury St. Edmunds extended to visits to The National Archives at Kew, London, where my accumulated photos of documents numbered over a thousand. Such photos were not allowed in the early days, but rules have since been relaxed. Another change has been the increased accessibility of online archive material, such as newspapers and genealogy, allowing me to supplement my research between work and family life. Less time travelling, meant more time researching. Perhaps the most rewarding development has been to connect with Pat's niece, and Susan's daughter, Anna. Throughout the writing of this book, I have kept Anna updated, and following the passing of Susan, custodianship of Pat's grave was passed to Anna. Anna, also dismayed that Pat has no headstone, is now empowered to have one installed. With a new headstone, and the publication of this book, Pat's getting the tributes she rightly deserves.

I have tried my luck at getting Pat a memorial of some kind. A few years back, I even approached the Commonwealth War Graves Commission to see if she qualified, because I knew civilian victims of war are commemorated by them. The response was civilians are commemorated if they were killed as a result of enemy action, as an internee, or by an Allied weapon of war. I have nothing but respect for the CWGC, and in no way do I ever wish them to dilute their remit, but I tried to claim Wyeth's bayonet was classed as an Allied weapon of war, even though I had no evidence to provide that he used one. Quite rightly, my spurious suggestion was declined. I have also occasionally reproduced snippets of Pat's story onto local social media pages, which has always generated huge interest, with people often voicing their support for a permanent memorial. After I visited Pat's grave in 2019, a local newspaper, the Eastern Daily Press, carried a full page featuring my research into the story, again sparking interest in the local community.

In 2022, after finally piecing together the full extent of this story, I considered the prospect of putting my research into a book, where I hoped Pat's story could reach a much wider audience. Mind you, this story had grown to be bigger than being just about Pat. It was also about how, during wartime, someone with a history of violence toward girls, could become a soldier and evade mental health treatment, to then find themself alone in a park with a six-year-old girl. It is also interesting to see how his actions were viewed by his peers, at a time when attitudes toward mental health were beginning to be more sympathetic. Some wanted him to hang, others preferred treatment over punishment. In October 2022, I typed the first words for my book, a book that was finally finished in March 2024. Its publishing was paid for by redundancy money I had put away a few years prior, an emergency fund for 'a rainy day'. Sometimes, those insignificant moments in time fit a larger jigsaw, until one day you fit that final piece.

I hope I have done Pat justice. The increasing number of people who know her name, from the story I have told, leads me to think I have. I will forever hold her dear in my heart, as do many others now. Bless you Pat.

ACKNOWLEDGEMENTS

Suffolk Archives, Bury St. Edmunds (formerly Bury St. Edmunds Records Office), 77 Raingate Street, Bury St. Edmunds, Suffolk, IP33 2AR – where it all started.

The National Archives (TNA). My gratitude to the staff for the swift handling of my Freedom of Information requests and responses to permission requests for reproducing copyright images. For those interested, here are the documents I reference in the writing of this book:

DPP21018 – Director of Prosecutions, James Wyeth's appeal.

DPP2987 – Director of Prosecutions, Chief Inspector Thomas Barratts notes, psychiatric reports on James Wyeth, Wyeth's juvenile record.

MEPO 3-2216 – Metropolitan Police, court papers, forensic images, statements, Wyeth's appeal, Chief Inspector Thomas Barratt's finished report.

PCOM9705 – Police Commission, Wyeth's juvenile record.

Norfolk Record Office (Norwich), The Archive Centre, Martineau Lane, Norwich, NR1 2DQ. The NRO holds the Norwich prison archive.

HMP 1/33 – Prison register.

HMP 7/5 – Governor's journals.

HMP 26/1 – Medical Officer Papers.

The British Newspaper Archive
(britishnewspaperarchive.co.uk) – subscription required.

Ancestry (ancestry.co.uk) – subscription required.

I owe a debt to my volunteer proofreaders. Each received an email of each chapter as I finished it, and it is through their much-valued feedback, triggering many revisions, I improved my writing style to make me the best version of a writer I could be. Thank you all. Geoffrey Herschell, Martin Lankester and Emma Sears. A special mention for Laina West, for her in-depth feedback and insights of book publishing. Check out Laina's books on Amazon. Also, a mention to Harri Aston, professional editor, for his thorough revisions and making me the best version of an author I could be. My gratitude to Jasmine Higgins, who helped design the book's cover, and Nathan and Maddy at Softwood Books, all who have helped transform my research into a book.

I will be eternally grateful for the assistance of Patricia's family, who at this moment in time I have yet to meet. The late Susan Cupit, Pat's sister, for supplying me with a photograph of Pat, and Anna Allan, Pat's niece, for her enthusiasm of what I am doing. Anna's praise for the book in Pat's memory, ensured I never gave up, even in those times I doubted myself. Thank you.

My wife, Sue, who has supported my need to lock myself away and tap away on a keyboard for hours to create the story of a girl murdered decades ago. Together, we have visited Pat's grave, and not once did she question why. Even as she stood in the cemetery, in the pouring rain, watching me trapse across unmarked graves searching for Pat's final resting place, not once did she urge me to stop. Nor did she leave my side for shelter. She stayed to watch me, then waited until I was done. It's those simple acts of support that mean the world. To my wife, I thank you the most.

Pat's headstone, May 2024. Image courtesy of Delphine Evon.